Teach Yourself VISUALLY™

Wireless Networking

2nd Edition

Visual®

by Rob Tidrow

WILEY

Wiley Publishing, Inc.

Teach Yourself VISUALLY™ Wireless Networking, 2nd Edition

Published by
Wiley Publishing, Inc.
111 River Street
Hoboken, NJ 07030-5774

Published simultaneously in Canada

Library of Congress Control Number: 2006927781

ISBN-13: 978-0-470-072691
ISBN-10: 0-470-07269-5
Manufactured in the United States of America

10 9 8 7 6 5 4 3 2 1

Trademark Acknowledgments

Contact Us

For general information on our other products and services please contact our Customer Care Department within the U.S. at 800-762-2974, outside the U.S. at 317-572-3993 or fax 317-572-4002.

For technical support please visit www.wiley.com/techsupport.

Wiley Publishing, Inc.

Sales

Contact Wiley
at (800) 762-2974 or
fax (317) 572-4002.

Praise for Visual Books

"Like a lot of other people, I understand things best when I see them visually. Your books really make learning easy and life more fun."

John T. Frey (Cadillac, MI)

"I have quite a few of your Visual books and have been very pleased with all of them. I love the way the lessons are presented!"

Mary Jane Newman (Yorba Linda, CA)

"I just purchased my third Visual book (my first two are dog-eared now!), and, once again, your product has surpassed my expectations."

Tracey Moore (Memphis, TN)

"I am an avid fan of your Visual books. If I need to learn anything, I just buy one of your books and learn the topic in no time. Wonders! I have even trained my friends to give me Visual books as gifts."

Illona Bergstrom (Aventura, FL)

"Thank you for making it so clear. I appreciate it. I will buy many more Visual books."

J.P. Sangdong (North York, Ontario, Canada)

"I have several books from the Visual series and have always found them to be valuable resources."

Stephen P. Miller (Ballston Spa, NY)

"Thank you for the wonderful books you produce. It wasn't until I was an adult that I discovered how I learn – visually. Nothing compares to Visual books. I love the simple layout. I can just grab a book and use it at my computer, lesson by lesson. And I understand the material! You really know the way I think and learn. Thanks so much!"

Stacey Han (Avondale, AZ)

"I absolutely admire your company's work. Your books are terrific. The format is perfect, especially for visual learners like me. Keep them coming!"

Frederick A. Taylor, Jr. (New Port Richey, FL)

"I have several of your Visual books and they are the best I have ever used."

Stanley Clark (Crawfordville, FL)

"I bought my first Teach Yourself VISUALLY book last month. Wow. Now I want to learn everything in this easy format!"

Tom Vial (New York, NY)

"Thank you, thank you, thank you...for making it so easy for me to break into this high-tech world. I now own four of your books. I recommend them to anyone who is a beginner like myself."

Gay O'Donnell (Calgary, Alberta, Canada)

"I write to extend my thanks and appreciation for your books. They are clear, easy to follow, and straight to the point. Keep up the good work! I bought several of your books and they are just right! No regrets! I will always buy your books because they are the best."

Seward Kollie (Dakar, Senegal)

"Compliments to the chef!! Your books are extraordinary! Or, simply put, extra-ordinary, meaning way above the rest! THANK YOU THANK YOU THANK YOU! I buy them for friends, family, and colleagues."

Christine J. Manfrin (Castle Rock, CO)

"What fantastic teaching books you have produced! Congratulations to you and your staff. You deserve the Nobel Prize in Education in the Software category. Thanks for helping me understand computers."

Bruno Tonon (Melbourne, Australia)

"Over time, I have bought a number of your 'Read Less - Learn More' books. For me, they are THE way to learn anything easily. I learn easiest using your method of teaching."

José A. Mazón (Cuba, NY)

"I am an avid purchaser and reader of the Visual series, and they are the greatest computer books I've seen. The Visual books are perfect for people like myself who enjoy the computer, but want to know how to use it more efficiently. Your books have definitely given me a greater understanding of my computer, and have taught me to use it more effectively. Thank you very much for the hard work, effort, and dedication that you put into this series."

Alex Diaz (Las Vegas, NV)

Credits

Project Editors
Tim Borek
Maureen Spears

Acquisitions Editor
Jody Lefevere

**Product Development
Supervisor**
Courtney Allen

Copy Editor
Kim Heusel

Technical Editor
Justin Kamm

Editorial Manager
Robyn Siesky

Business Manager
Amy Knies

Manufacturing
Allan Conley
Linda Cook
Paul Gilchrist
Jennifer Guynn

Editorial Assistant
Laura Sinise

Book Design
Kathie S. Rickard

Production Coordinator
Adrienne Martinez

Layout
Jennifer Mayberry
Heather Ryan
Amanda Spagnuolo

Screen Artist
Jill A. Proll

Illustrators
Ronda David-Burroughs
Cheryl Grubbs
Jake Mansfield

Proofreader
Sossity R. Smith

Quality Control
Brian H. Walls

Indexer
Johnna Van Hoose

**Vice President and Executive
Group Publisher**
Richard Swadley

Vice President and Publisher
Barry Pruett

Composition Director
Debbie Stailey

About the Author

Rob Tidrow is a technical writer and has authored or co-authored over 30 books on a wide variety of computer and technical topics, including Microsoft Windows XP, Microsoft Outlook 2003, Windows 2000 Server, and Microsoft Internet Information Server. Some of his previous works include *Master Visually Windows XP Service Pack 2 Edition*, and *Wireless Networking Quick Tips*. Rob currently is a Technical Communicator for Ontario Systems in Muncie, Indiana. He lives in Centerville, Indiana, with his wife Tammy and their two sons, Adam and Wesley. You can reach him via e-mail at robtidrow@yahoo.com.

Author's Acknowledgments

What a ride! This book was fun to write and put together. I want to thank everyone at Wiley Publishing for helping put together this book. Many kudos go to Maureen Spears to help drive this book along—and to prod me along. Big thanks to Jody Lefevere for thinking of me when this book became available. To Kim Heusel and Justin Kamm, I would like to say thank you for copy editing and technically reviewing this book. Also, thanks to Barry Pruett for sticking with me through all these long years.

Table of Contents

chapter 1   Introducing Wireless Networking

chapter 2   Setting Up Wireless Network Hardware

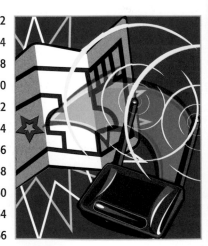

chapter 3 Installing Wireless Hardware in PCs

chapter 4 Configuring Wireless Networks

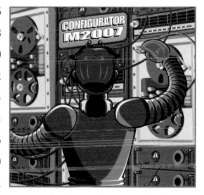

chapter 5 Creating Computer-to-Computer Networks

Table of Contents

chapter 6 — Software for Wireless Computing

chapter 7 — Communicating with Wireless Computers

chapter 8 — Using Wireless Computers for Business Presentations

chapter 9 Using Wireless Computers for Entertainment

chapter 10 Working on Wireless Networks

Table of Contents

chapter 13 Connecting on the Road

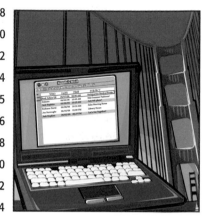

chapter 14 Improving Network Performance

chapter 15 Troubleshooting a Wireless Network

How to use this book

Do you look at the pictures in a book or newspaper before anything else on a page? Would you rather see an image instead of read about how to do something? Search no further. This book is for you. Opening *Teach Yourself VISUALLY Wireless Networking, 2nd Edition* allows you to read less and learn more about building and maintaining your out wireless network.

Who Needs This Book

This book is for a reader who has never used this particular technology. It is also for more computer literate individuals who want to expand their knowledge of the different features that wireless networking has to offer.

Book Organization

Teach Yourself VISUALLY Wireless Networking, 2nd Edition has 15 chapters.

Chapter 1, **Introducing Wireless Networking**, helps you discover the wireless world and includes sections on the benefits of going wireless, system requirements, network standards, and more.

Chapter 2, **Setting Up Wireless Network Hardware**, shows you how to select the right hardware for your system, how to configure broadband modems, network bridges, and residential gateways, as well as how to set up wireless gateways and access points. It also covers downloading and updating firmware, and setting up DHCP.

Chapter 3, **Installing Wireless Hardware in PCs**, covers how to install and configure network adapters, how to confirm driver installation, and how to update adapter firmware.

Chapter 4, **Configuring Wireless Networks**, shows you the available networks, as well as how to configure, add, remove, or move a preferred network. You also learn how to view the signal strength, and how to create a wireless bridge.

Chapter 5, **Creating Computer-to-Computer Networks**, shows you how to configure a host PC and a client PC, and how to enable Internet sharing.

In Chapter 6, **Software for Wireless Computing**, you learn about Office Suites, e-mail applications, and Web browsers. You also find out how to transfer and synchronize files.

Chapter 7, **Communicating with Wireless Computers**, covers the different types of communication software, including e-mail and Web mail.

In Chapter 8, **Using Wireless Computers for Business Presentations**, you learn how to create and present a slide show.

Chapter 9, **Using Wireless Computers for Entertainment**, you learn how to register for online music as well as how to download music for your enjoyment. You also learn about Weblogs, Streaming Radio, and Online Gaming.

In Chapter 10, **Working on Wireless Networks**, you discover how to connect to a wireless network, browse a network, and create and monitor a shared folder. You also discover how to assign a letter to a network folder and how to add a network printer.

In Chapter 11, **Administering Wireless Networks**, you find out how to establish, add, and delete a user account. You also learn how to assign a user password, how to activate a Guest account, change a workgroup name, as well as how to share information and printers on a wireless network.

Chapter 12, **Securing Wireless Networks**, covers the various threats to network security and how to enable and manage various technologies, including WEP encryption, hardware access lists, and firewalls, to prevent theft of information.

In Chapter 13, **Connecting on the Road**, you discover the benefits of having a mobile computer, including how to purchase the best computer for your needs, find the best service providers, monitor battery life, connect away from home, find hotspots and available networks, and set up a VPN connection.

Chapter 14, **Improving Network Performance**, you learn about the factors that affect wireless range, how to increase that range, and how to monitor radio signals.

Chapter 15, **Troubleshooting a Wireless Network**, shows you how to troubleshoot the problems you may encounter with your network using various diagnostic tools.

Chapter Organization

This book consists of sections, all listed in the book's table of contents. A *section* is a set of steps that show you how to complete a specific computer task.

Each section, usually contained on two facing pages, has an introduction to the task at hand, a set of full-color screen shots and steps that walk you through the task, and a set of tips. This format allows you to quickly look at a topic of interest and learn it instantly.

Chapters group together three or more sections with a common theme. A chapter may also contain pages that give you the background information needed to understand the sections in a chapter.

What You Need to Use This Book

Using the Mouse

This book uses the following conventions to describe the actions you perform when using the mouse:

Click

Press your left mouse button once. You generally click your mouse on something to select something on the screen.

Double-click

Press your left mouse button twice. Double-clicking something on the computer screen generally opens whatever item you have double-clicked.

Right-click

Press your right mouse button. When you right-click anything on the computer screen, the program displays a shortcut menu containing commands specific to the selected item.

Click and Drag, and Release the Mouse

Move your mouse pointer and hover it over an item on the screen. Press and hold down the left mouse button. Now, move the mouse to where you want to place the item and then release the button. You use this method to move an item from one area of the computer screen to another.

The Conventions in This Book

A number of typographic and layout styles have been used throughout *Teach Yourself VISUALLY Wireless Networking, 2nd Edition* to distinguish different types of information.

Bold

Bold type represents the names of commands and options that you interact with. Bold type also indicates text and numbers that you must type into a dialog box or window.

Italics

Italic words introduce a new term and are followed by a definition.

Numbered Steps

You must perform the instructions in numbered steps in order to successfully complete a section and achieve the final results.

Bulleted Steps

These steps point out various optional features. You do not have to perform these steps; they simply give additional information about a feature.

Indented Text

Indented text tells you what the program does in response to you following a numbered step. For example, if you click a certain menu command, a dialog box may appear, or a window may open. Indented text may also tell you what the final result is when you follow a set of numbered steps.

Notes

Notes give additional information. They may describe special conditions that may occur during an operation. They may warn you of a situation that you want to avoid, for example the loss of data. A note may also cross reference a related area of the book. A cross reference may guide you to another chapter, or another section with the current chapter.

Icons and buttons

Icons and buttons are graphical representations within the text. They show you exactly what you need to click to perform a step.

 You can easily identify the tips in any section by looking for the TIPS icon. Tips offer additional information, including tips, hints, and tricks. You can use the TIPS information to go beyond what you have learn learned in the steps.

Introducing Wireless Networking

Wireless networks allow you to connect computers together and access the Internet without wires or cables. You can use wireless networks in businesses of all types and sizes, the military, schools, churches, and municipalities. Today, workers can connect to workplace networks and remain in contact with other workers through e-mail, Web sites, file sharing, and shared calendaring even when physically away from the office. This chapter discusses the different types of wireless networks and other important issues, such as security concerns.

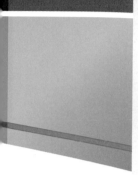

Discover Wireless Networks

A wireless network enables a group of connected computers and devices to communicate without being physically connected to a network. It eliminates the cables used in wired networks. The most popular wireless networks are called *Wi-Fi*, or Wireless Fidelity, networks.

One of the main problems in the past with wireless networks has been the speed with which users could communicate with each other. Because of new standards and emerging technologies, wireless networks now have similar connectivity speeds as hard-wired networks.

Radio Signals

Wireless networks use radio signals, similar to those in radio and television broadcasting, to transmit data between devices. Wi-Fi networks operate on the 2.4 GHz or 5 GHz frequency band. These networks can send data at speeds up to 54 Mbps (megabits per second).

Radio Transceivers

A radio transceiver sends and receives radio signals. Each device in a wireless network has a radio transceiver to send and receive information to and from the network. A transceiver can be located inside or outside a computer.

Mobility of Network

You can move laptop computers and other wireless-enabled devices while remaining connected to the network. Depending on the technology and other factors, a wireless network has a range of 150 to 350 feet. In addition, as a laptop computer user, you can connect to other wireless networks while traveling.

Speed

The faster the network speed, the faster that files and other data move from one computer to another computer. Newer wireless network technologies enable faster data transmission than some wired networks. However, Fast Ethernet and gigabit Ethernet networks can move at least twice the data of the fastest wireless network technologies.

Cost

Prices for wireless networking equipment are rapidly falling, making it possible to create an inexpensive, fast, and reliable wireless network. While wired networks can be much faster, they often involve intrusive wiring throughout a home or office.

Understanding What a Network Is

A network comprises many different components. Some of these components include a network adapter — also called a network interface card, or NIC — cables, routers, servers, hubs, switches, and network operating systems.

Communication

Networks enable different computers and devices to exchange information such as files and documents. If a network is connected to the Internet, the network also enables connected devices to access information available on the Internet. A network can consist of many different components or as few as two.

Infrastructure

The *infrastructure* of a network is the term used to describe the physical bits and pieces across which information travels. Cabling, routers, hubs, and switches are all considered part of the network infrastructure. A small home network can consist of very few components, while large networks can consist of thousands of pieces of equipment and require a full-time team of personnel to maintain it.

Access Points

Access points are the locations on a network that provide access to the network for devices and computers. When used with wireless technology, a network can use a single access point to allow multiple wireless devices to access the network.

Servers

Servers are computers that are dedicated to performing one or a few tasks on a network. Most business networks use dedicated servers for services such as file storage, Internet access, and running applications such as a database program. It is possible to run multiple servers on one physical computer. For example, a single computer on a network may be an e-mail server and a Web server at the same time.

Clients

Clients are computers that require services from the network. Most computers require communication with network servers using applications called *client applications*. For example, a Web browser is the client application for accessing information from a Web server.

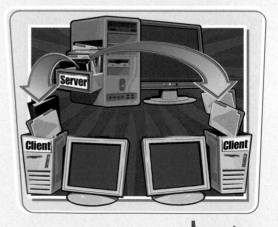

continued

Peripherals

A *peripheral* refers to the devices you can connect either directly to the network or to computers that are connected to a network. Once you have connected a device to a network, anyone on the network can access the device with the appropriate authorization. Some examples of the numerous types of devices you can connect to a network are printers, scanners, storage devices, and cameras.

Topology

The *topology* of a network determines the physical layout of the network. The most common topology is the star topology that has a device such as a hub or router as the center of the *star*, connected to different devices. Other lesser-used topologies are the *bus* and the *tree* topologies.

Backbone

The *backbone* of a network is the term used to describe the main cable within a network where most network traffic transverses. A backbone is typically connected to many other devices such as routers and switches, rather than to single computers. The backbone of a network must be able to handle large amounts of information or bandwidth. Large networks typically use fiber-optic cables and very fast network devices.

Network Protocols

Computers and other devices connected to a network can communicate with each other because they all agree to use the same method of exchanging information called a *protocol*. A network can use many different protocols simultaneously. For example, a Web browser communicates with a Web site using a protocol that specifies how Web information is exchanged, while two network cards exchange messages over a cable using a different protocol that dictates how information is transmitted via electrical signals on a cable.

Cables

Apart from very simple wireless networks, all networks contain cabling, which exchanges information between computers and devices such as switches. The most common type of cable is *twisted-pair* cable, which contains four pairs of wires (eight wires total) that are entwined with each other. The end of the cable terminates with a connector in the shape of a large telephone connector.

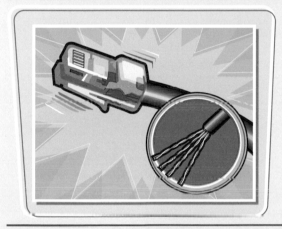

Size

The size of a network determines how the network is referenced. A network within a single building is called a *local area network*, or *LAN*. Networks that connect across a larger area or even across a country are called *wide area networks*, or *WANs*. LANs that contain wireless technologies are referred to as *Wireless LANs*, or *WLANs*.

Discover the Benefits of Wireless Networking

Both businesses and homes are using wireless networks more and more because you can easily become mobile and still access network resources at the same time. A corporate manager, for example, can carry her laptop computer to a scheduling meeting and access e-mails, shared calendars, and other resources using the wireless network, eliminating network cable connections.

You can also become mobile using handheld devices, such as a personal digital assistant (PDA), which are small devices that you carry in a pocket, purse, or hip holder, and that include software for accessing e-mail, Web services, shared files, and more.

Remain Mobile

One of the major benefits of wireless networking is being able to remain mobile while using a computer, but still have access to all the services and resources made available from a network, such as the Internet. You can even use a laptop computer while you move in a car or plane, as long as the computer is in range of the wireless network.

Fast Setup

Once you set up the infrastructure for a wireless network, you can add more computers and devices to the network quickly. Once you add a wireless network adapter to a computer and configure the computer to use wireless networking, the computer can connect to the network immediately.

Cost

As opposed to networks that use cables, wireless networks can be much cheaper to set up. Apart from the costs associated with equipment like hubs and repeaters, the installation of cable through an existing building may be very difficult and expensive. Wireless networks also allow networks to transverse objects, such as roads, that require a lot of work and money to cross with cables.

Easy to Move

In traditional networks that require the use of cable, you cannot easily move a computer to a new location, because you must attach the computer to a nearby outlet using a cable. It is sometimes difficult to move a network computer to a new location within the same room. A wireless network allows you to move any computer anywhere, so long as the computer is in range of the wireless network.

Expandability

Adding a new computer or device to a wireless network is as simple as turning the computer on. Most wireless devices, such as access points, can support many different devices, and so long as you do not exceed the maximum number of devices, the access point quickly accepts new connections. If needed, you can add multiple access points to a wireless network to facilitate large numbers of computers.

Understanding the Disadvantages of Wireless Networking

While wireless networks have a wide range of benefits, some unique disadvantages include speed, battery life of mobile devices, interference, security issues, cost, and interruptions in services. Organizations that rely on wireless networks must test for and fix problems in areas where buildings or stronger radio signals may interfere with transmissions.

Because wireless networks use radio frequencies, it is difficult to prevent breaches in security. Companies must use access privileges to control access to a network via a wireless device so that only authorized people and devices can access the network.

Power Consumption

Each wireless device in a computer, such as a laptop or a handheld computer, has a radio transmitter and receiver. Radio devices require a relatively large amount of power to operate effectively. Using wireless adapters on portable devices can greatly reduce the length of time that the devices can operate using battery power.

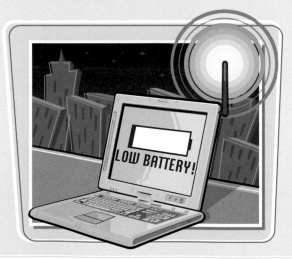

Interference

Wireless networks use radio signals to transmit information. Unfortunately, there are many types of devices that use radio waves to operate. These other devices can interfere with the signals that the wireless network uses. Tracking down and eliminating interference sources can be difficult.

Network Security

By their very nature, wireless networks are more susceptible to unauthorized access. A network may be accessible from a location not under the control of a network administrator, such as a parking lot next to the building housing the wireless network. While cable networks have the same concerns, they are not as easy to access as wireless networks.

Inconsistent Connections

With cable networks, computers are ensured a direct, stable connection to the network. However, moving a computer to another location or items blocking the path of transmission can interrupt wireless network connections. While many applications, such as Web browsing, are adversely affected by temporary connection loss, other applications, such as database-based applications, may result in information loss.

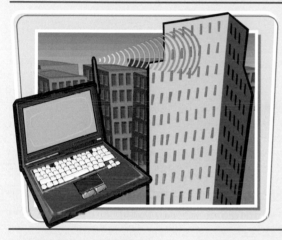

Lack of Management

With a wired network, network administrators can exercise very tight control of the physical components of the network. For example, network administrators can ensure that all cables are the correct distance from devices that may cause disruptions, such as light systems or photocopiers. With wireless networks, short of physically inspecting each wireless device, there is no way that administrators can determine or control the exact physical layout of the network.

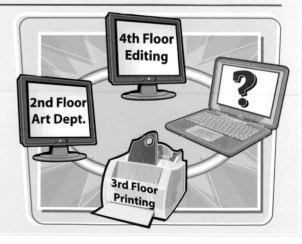

4th Floor
Editing

2nd Floor
Art Dept.

3rd Floor
Printing

Discover the Types of Wireless Technology

Wireless technology enables computers and devices to communicate with each other without the use of wires. There are many different types of wireless technologies, each one with its own set of strengths and weaknesses.

Companies or municipalities may settle on one or several types of technology for their network depending on their needs. For example, a company that has a campus setting with several buildings may use microwave and infrared. The microwave technology can transfer data from building to building, while your infrared devices transfer data inside the building.

Wi-Fi

Wireless Fidelity, or *Wi-Fi*, is becoming the preferred technology for creating wireless networks both at home and at work. Wi-Fi allows computers and devices, such as printers and hubs, to communicate without using cables. Most new wireless networking devices in use are Wi-Fi devices. Wi-Fi is also used to facilitate Internet access in public places, such as airports.

Bluetooth

Bluetooth is the name of the wireless technology that is used primarily to allow individual devices to communicate with each other over short distances. For example, handheld computers can transmit a phone number from an address book to a mobile phone, which then dials the number. While possible, Bluetooth is not generally used to network computers together.

Infrared

Wireless infrared technology allows two devices to communicate using infrared light and you most commonly find them in remote controls. Infrared devices need to maintain a constant line of sight between the devices and are more reliable over short distances. The most common use of infrared technology is allowing handheld computers to exchange data with each other and laptop computers. Most handheld devices and laptops have a built-in infrared port.

Cellular

Cellular wireless technology is most commonly associated with mobile telephones. Each telephone communicates with a nearby transmitter, which changes as the phone moves around a location. Laptop computers routinely use cellular phones as modems to provide dial-up access from remote locations.

Microwave

Microwave technology enables two devices to communicate using microwave dishes that are aligned with each other. You can use microwave systems to connect the networks of two buildings that are separated by obstructions such as wide roads. Microwave systems are very expensive but can transfer large amounts of information.

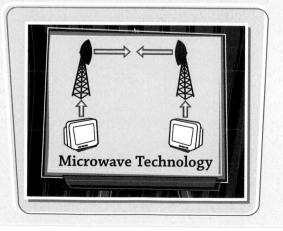

Discover Applications for Wireless Networks

Wireless networks increase the efficiency of many specific applications, making them extremely useful when you use them with wireless networking.

By far, the main application for wireless networking is person-to-person communication. All types of users use e-mail, messaging applications and scheduling software, from the president of a Fortune 500 company sending quarterly company results, to youth baseball coaches sending messages to players about upcoming practices.

E-mail

E-mail is by far the most popular networking application, and wireless networking now makes it possible to access e-mail constantly. You can use laptop computers, and, increasingly, handheld computers, to access e-mail wirelessly at work and elsewhere with more frequency at public locations, such as airports and cafes.

Messaging

Most operating systems provide a messaging application that allows you to communicate instantly using text. Even inexpensive handhelds now have the capability to provide messaging services and, when coupled with wireless networking, allow you to stay in constant communication with your colleagues and friends wherever you are.

Scheduling

The ability for people to schedule activities and notify others of their activities greatly increases the efficiency with which they can work together. Allowing workers to update their schedules and exchange that information immediately using wireless technologies only further increases the efficiency of the scheduling system.

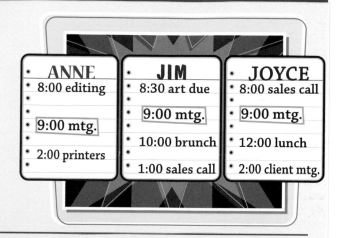

ANNE	JIM	JOYCE
8:00 editing	8:30 art due	8:00 sales call
9:00 mtg.	9:00 mtg.	9:00 mtg.
2:00 printers	10:00 brunch	12:00 lunch
	1:00 sales call	2:00 client mtg.

Pieces of cake in stock: 2

Data Collection

Making computers mobile increases the speed at which you can update data in applications such as inventory control systems. For example, a person in the warehouse can immediately update information about the number of products on a shelf instead of waiting until one has access to a computer.

Web Browsing

For most home users, the primary use of wireless networks is the ability to use a mobile computer, such as a laptop, to connect to the Internet regardless of where they are in the house. Most wireless networks used at home are easily connected to the Internet and can provide access not only in the house, but also in the area outside of the house, such as a deck or patio.

WWW Porch — WWW Den
WWW Kitchen — WWW Bedroom
Floor Plan

To connect to a wireless network, you must equip your computer with minimal hardware and software when connecting it to a wireless network. You should also review system requirements to ensure your computer, handheld device, or other component meets the wireless networking standards that your company, school, or home use.

This is analogous to you speaking English and your friend speaking Spanish; one or the other must be able to understand and speak the other person's language or your communication shuts down.

Operating System

You need a PC running Microsoft Windows XP, either the Home or the Professional version. Windows XP is an operating system that controls your computer. Windows XP has built-in wireless networking support that makes it easy to create and maintain wireless networks. However, you do not need Windows XP to go wireless.

Hardware

You must equip your desktop PC or a laptop computer with a Pentium 4 1.2 GHz processor, 256 megabytes of memory, and a 40GB hard drive.

PC Ports

You need to install some basic networking equipment on your computer. To start, your computer needs some empty slots where the equipment is connected. Your desktop PC should have an available PCI slot. Your laptop computer should have a PC card slot. If neither of these is available, it is also possible to use the USB port with some equipment. For more information about attaching networking equipment to your computer, see Chapter 3. One advantage of using USB ports for networking equipment is the ease at which you can connect the equipment. With USB, you simply plug in the equipment, such as a network interface adapter. You do not have to open up the computer case to make the connection.

Internet Access

If you want to connect to the Internet with your wireless network, you need Internet access. To get the full benefit of a wireless network, you need high-speed, or broadband, access. This is available through a local telephone company's DSL service or a cable TV system's cable modem service. You can access the Internet directly or through another computer if that computer is using the Internet Connection Sharing feature available with Microsoft Windows XP.

Consider Your Networking Requirements

Before deciding the type of wireless network to build, consider how many computers will connect to the network and what operations you want the network to provide. You can do this by taking inventory of the types of services, applications, and connections you use now, and then adapt those things that can go wireless into your wireless network design.

For example, if you currently use e-mail, scheduling, data warehousing, and spreadsheet applications, consider making all those available over the wireless network. You can store your spreadsheets, for example, on a central server that you can access by wired and wireless computers.

Set Up Home or Office

The simplest wireless network is one home computer connected to a broadband Internet connection. In a larger family, there may be several desktop and laptop PCs connecting to the Internet and to each other through a wireless network. In an office environment, you may want to choose one of the newer, faster networking technologies that use the 802.11g standard.

Number of Computers

The number of desktop PCs, laptop computers, and other network-enabled devices determines how much wireless networking equipment like routers and network interface cards — NICs — you need to purchase, install, and configure. Your wireless network may consist of one to dozens of computers connecting to the Internet and to each other.

Mobile Access

If you want to access wireless networks while traveling, you need a laptop PC or personal digital assistant, or PDA. These devices let you connect to available Wi-Fi hot spots in many places you visit. You also can use the devices to connect to your wireless network when you are at home or in your office. Laptops come in several different varieties, including lightweight, durable, high-performance, large screen, and so on. The one you pick should match the type of work you plan to do. For example, if you travel a great deal and want a lightweight model, look for one that weighs 4-6 pounds. However, if you need a high-performance laptop that can handle graphics-intensive software, you may need to opt for a heavier laptop that weighs over 10 pounds.

Mixing Wi-Fi Standards

If you connect computers and equipment that use multiple standards, you need *dual-band* capability. This allows you to mix and match wireless technologies. For example, if one network uses equipment with the 802.11a standard and another operates under the 802.11b standard, you can connect them together using a dual-band router.

Discover Wireless Standards

The most popular wireless networking technologies today are based on the 802.11 standard, which governs how devices on the network communicate with each other. Popularly known as Wi-Fi, the Institute of Electrical and Electronic Engineers (IEEE) developed the standard, of which there are several variations.

When you set up purchasing requirements for your home or office wireless network infrastructure, take the time to understand the wireless standards that each component supports. If you use Wi-Fi, for example, all your components that connect to that Wi-Fi device must be Wi-Fi compatible.

Wi-Fi

Wi-Fi stands for *Wireless Fidelity*. It now generally refers to all the 802.11 wireless networking standards, which specify how devices communicate using wireless networks, although it originally identified networks that used the 802.11b standard. The Wi-Fi Alliance, a nonprofit industry association, works to ensure interoperability among the various 802.11 wireless technology standards.

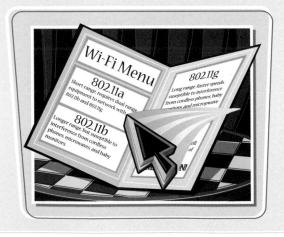

802.11a

The 802.11a standard is the least popular of the Wi-Fi technologies. While it is beneficial for some office networks with high-bandwidth needs and closely located computers, it has a short range. Dual-range equipment allows 802.11a equipment to network with the more popular 802.11b standard and the newer 802.11g standard. Otherwise, the 802.11a standard is incompatible with the 802.11b and 802.11g standards.

802.11b

The 802.11b standard is the most popular of the Wi-Fi technologies. It transmits data at a slower speed than both the 802.11a and 802.11g standards. Unlike 802.11a networks, 802.11b radio waves can penetrate most walls, but are susceptible to interference from cordless phones, baby monitors, and microwave ovens.

802.11g

The 802.11g is the newest Wi-Fi standard with the same range as the 802.11b standard but with the ability to transmit data at a much faster rate. It can communicate with 802.11b networks, but requires dual-band equipment to interact with networks based on the 802.11a standard. It suffers from interference problems similar to networks using the 802.11b standard, such as cordless phones, baby monitors, and microwave ovens.

802.11i

The 802.11i is an emerging standard that will increase the security of Wi-Fi networks. When it is available, you may be able to upgrade some older equipment to this newer standard.

Discover Network Configurations

You must choose which type of wireless network configuration you need. *Configuration* is how the network is laid out to allow network computers to communicate with the server and each other. The two general types are infrastructure and computer-to-computer, or ad hoc. How you configure your network depends on the size of network, costs, resources you want to access, and the number of users.

Some wireless networks need a centralized access point that several computers will use to "jump" to a larger network – such as the Internet. Other wireless networks may be small enough where a single computer can act as a shared device that can then allow the other computers to access other networks.

INFRASTRUCTURE	COMPUTER TO COMPUTER
COMPUTERS ↓ ROUTER ↓ MODEM ↓ INTERNET	COMPUTERS ↓ MAIN COMPUTER ↓ INTERNET

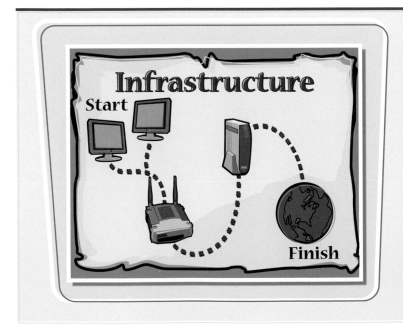

Infrastructure

An *infrastructure* network is the most widely used wireless network configuration. It uses a wireless router, also called an access point or gateway, to connect to the Internet through a broadband modem. The wireless router then communicates with other wireless-enabled devices on the network. Infrastructure networks can bridge wireless networks with existing wired, or Ethernet, networks.

Computer to Computer

A computer-to-computer, or *ad hoc*, network allows computers to communicate with each other without the use of an access point, such as a router. This basic network configuration permits you to exchange files among computers. In addition, one computer in a network can directly connect to the Internet and permit other computers to share the connection. Computer-to-computer networks are the easiest types of wireless networks to create and manage. As long as one computer is set up as a host computer, other computers can connect to the host as client computers. From there, all the computers on the network can communicate with each other, enabling them to share files, share printers, and communicate with e-mail.

Discover Networking Speeds

The speed of your network depends on many factors, such as the technology in use and your home or office layout. You may choose to use a technology that gives you a faster speed but less range.

Unfortunately, there are no wireless technologies available that allow extremely high speeds over great distances. At the present time, you can be several hundred feet away and get high-speed connections. However, as your distance increases, your speeds deteriorate and eventually fade out.

Reality Check

You will find that theoretical network speeds and real network speeds are not the same. Your wireless network's actual speed — that is, the rate at which it transfers data — depends on the distance between computers, which standard you choose, and the manufacturer of your equipment.

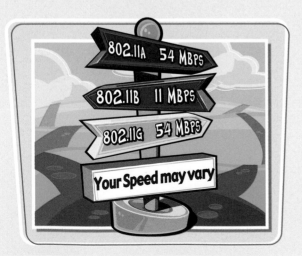

802.11a Speed

The 802.11a standard has a potential speed of 54 Mbps.

802.11b Speed

The 802.11b standard, the most popular wireless networking mode, has a potential speed of 11 Mbps.

802.11g Speed

The 802.11g standard, while operating in the same frequency band as the 802.11b standard, has a potential speed of 54 Mbps.

Ethernet Speeds

In contrast to wireless networking speeds, wired Ethernet networks are still the speed winners. Ethernets operate at only 10 Mbps, less than Wi-Fi speed. However, Fast Ethernets operate at 100 Mbps, and the newer gigabit Ethernets are even faster. While you gain in speed with the faster wired networks, you lose the freedom of mobility that Wi-Fi technology provides.

Estimate Coverage Range

The technology you use and your environment determine how far your wireless network can reach. Walls and metal structures reduce the range.

Planning for the coverage range of your wireless network is an inexact science. You can measure the distance between buildings, compare your location with others in your area, and research all the standards out there. However, you cannot determine exactly how far your wireless network reaches until you install it. You may end up relocating wireless switches and servers to eliminate or reduce obstacles.

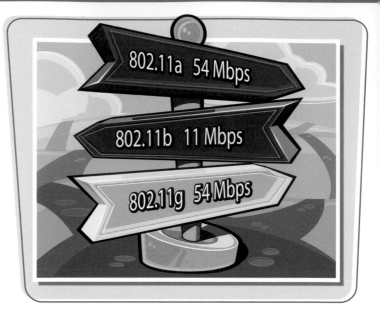

802.11a Range

Operating in the 5 GHz frequency range, the 802.11a standard is best suited for dense networks with high bandwidth needs. In a typical office environment, 802.11a networks have a possible range of up to 255 feet. The typical range is 25 to 75 feet indoors. Coverage is limited to one room.

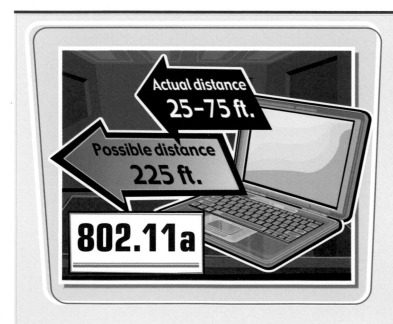

802.11b Range

Wireless networks operating on the 802.11b standard have a greater range than those using 802.11a. As the most popular standard, it often is used for public access locations, or hot spots. Its signals, operating in the 2.4 GHz frequency band, penetrate most walls and have a possible range of up to 300 feet. The typical range is up to 100 to 150 feet indoors.

802.11g Range

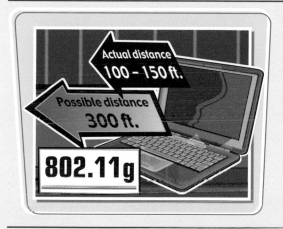

802.11g, the newest standard in the Wi-Fi networking family, has the same range as the 802.11b standard: up to 300 feet, but typically 100 to 150 feet indoors. However, it is much faster than networks using the 802.11b standard. Operating in the 2.4 GHz frequency range, 802.11g network signals can penetrate most walls. This allows homes and small businesses to add 802.11g devices in central locations and provide wireless access to most of their users. In addition, because of the high connection speeds of 802.11g devices, multiple computers can connect to the same 802.11g device (such as a router) without noticeable performance issues.

Other Range Factors

Some cordless phones, baby monitors, and microwave ovens can interfere with Wi-Fi networks using the 802.11b and 802.11g standards, decreasing their range. Keep this in mind when you position your wireless networks around children's rooms, kitchens, and break rooms. You may also find that cellular phone towers interfere with your wireless devices. If you are near one of these towers and interference is an issue, consider using a combination of conventional wired devices and wireless devices for your network.

Setting Up Wireless Network Hardware

Before you create a wireless network, you should know about the different types of networking hardware. This chapter shows how to install and configure routers and other wireless networking hardware. In many respects, wireless networking hardware is the same as conventional wired networking hardware, but wireless hardware uses devices that can receive and transmit radio waves, delivering packets of digital data.

Understanding Wireless Hardware Installation Issues

To properly install and set up your wireless hardware, you must consider several issues. This includes always referring to the equipment documentation before installation and setup. You must also try to anticipate where users will most likely congregate to access the network when you install hardware.

Remember to include wireless access points in conference rooms, and to place the devices in the most centralized locations. Consider attaching them to the ceiling of the room so they are up and out of the way, but so that users can access them.

Location

When installing wireless hardware, pay special attention to the location of the equipment. For example, placing a wireless access point in the middle of a basement may give better coverage throughout the house than if you place the access point in the corner of the basement. If you expect to use the upper floors in the house frequently, you may consider placing the access point on the first floor instead of the basement.

Cabling

Some wireless equipment, such as routers, can have standard Ethernet network ports on them to enable a computer to connect directly to the wireless device by using a network cable. If you plan to install a wireless device next to a computer that will use the device, look for wireless equipment with a network port so you can use standard, more inexpensive, cable instead of using wireless technology to span a short distance.

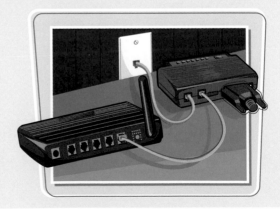

Ease of Access

You can position most network equipment in many ways, such as fastening them to a wall or stacking them on top of other network equipment. Unlike other nonwireless network devices, you may have to move wireless network equipment and even adjust the antenna from time to time as the wireless network changes. When positioning your network hardware, always give yourself plenty of room to work with the equipment.

Available Computer

Almost all wireless equipment requires the use of a computer to set up the initial hardware. Some devices require a connection to a computer with a network card and a network cable. The configuration software can then run on the computer, and you can use the software to adjust the settings on the wireless device. Once you configure the wireless device, you can detach the computer from the device.

Internet Access

Some applications, such as those that update the firmware on a hardware device, require that you have access to the Internet in order to obtain the necessary files to update the equipment. Before setting up your wireless device, check the hardware manufacturer's Web site to ensure that you have the latest version of any software to configure your hardware.

Settings

There are many different network settings that you may need to know to configure your wireless equipment; for example, computer names and IP addresses. Before setting up your wireless equipment, you should have available all the necessary information, including the Internet settings of your ISP if you want to connect the network to the Internet.

Select Wireless Hardware

At a minimum, your wireless infrastructure network requires a broadband modem and wireless residential gateway. Choosing the correct wireless hardware allows you to build a wireless network that fits your needs now and in the future.

Consider investing in backup or duplicate hardware in some instances, for example, additional wireless network adapters for your cache of laptops. Then, you can quickly replace any stolen, lost, or damaged laptops. This also provides duplicate hardware for any new laptops in the future.

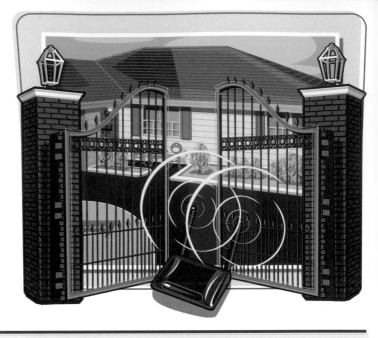

Broadband Modem

A *broadband modem* connects your wireless network to a high-speed Internet connection. Your broadband provider, which is usually your telephone or cable TV company, normally installs and configures this hardware for you. Some *residential gateways* include broadband modem functionality.

Residential Gateway

A wireless *residential gateway* is a hardware device that handles data traffic between your broadband modem and the computers on your network. A wireless residential gateway, which is one type of wireless *access point*, incorporates a *wireless router* that transmits and receives radio signals to and from wireless devices on your network. Wireless infrastructure networks require either a residential gateway or a wireless *access point*.

Access Point

You can use a wireless *access point*, or AP, to extend the range of your wireless network and fill in radio-signal coverage gaps. You also can use a wireless access point to connect a wireless device to your wired network without purchasing a residential gateway or router.

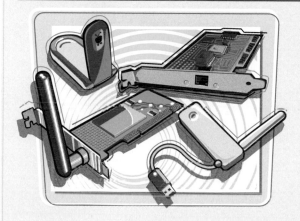

Network Adapter

Each computer or device on your wireless *network* requires a network adapter. Network adapters are also known as network interface cards — or NICs. For more information on network adapters, see Chapter 3.

Network Bridge

You typically use a *network bridge* to connect two networks together. You can also use a bridge to connect a device with a network port, such as a network printer to an existing wireless network. You do not typically use network bridges in home networks.

continued

Laptop Adapters

Most laptop computers have an expansion slot that you can use to add features such as a modem or network adapter to the laptop. The PC card slot on a laptop, sometimes referred to as the PCMCIA slot, can accept PC card wireless network adapters. Unfortunately, you must remove any existing PC card in order to install the wireless network card. Many newer laptops have a wireless interface built into them, leaving your PC card slots open and available for use for other accessories.

Handheld Adapters

Many handheld devices have a built-in slot called a *compact flash interface*. You can insert a network interface card in the slot in the same manner as inserting a card into a laptop. Despite the many uses of the compact flash slot, you must remove all cards, including memory cards, from the slot to use wireless networking. Although similar in size and shape to network cards in laptop computers, wireless network adapters in handheld computers are not compatible with laptop computers.

External Adapters

Wireless adapters are also available that you can connect to the USB port of a laptop or desktop computer. A USB wireless adapter makes it easy to move a network interface to multiple computers as needed. Most computers, including laptop computers, have a USB port that you can use to connect to a wireless adapter.

Built-In Wireless Networking

As wireless networks become more popular and standards become more accepted, more computer devices have wireless networking built in. Currently, most major manufacturers of handheld and laptop computers offer models with built-in wireless networking.

Game Adapters

Game consoles are dedicated gaming systems used in the home solely for playing games. You usually attach them to a television. Many game consoles have network connections that enable users to play games via the Internet or against users on another game console on the network. Some manufacturers are now creating wireless network adapters that are optimized for use with game consoles.

Personal Video Recorders

Personal Video Recorders (PVRs), sometimes called *Digital Video Recorders*, are the new generation of devices that record TV for later viewing. These devices are the next generation of VCRs. Some of these systems, such as certain models of TiVo, now offer wireless network capability to expand the abilities of the system.

Configure Broadband Modems

Most wireless networks are connected to a high-speed Internet connection using broadband modems, which are not really like the modem you use to connect your computer to a telephone line. Instead, cable modems convert (modulate and demodulate) cable television signals so your computer can access the Internet over cable.

You can purchase broadband modems, but most cable and DSL providers offer them as lease options when they set up your Internet connection. The advantage of leasing is you get updates to the equipment as they become available. The disadvantage is you may end paying more for the cost of the cable modem over the long run.

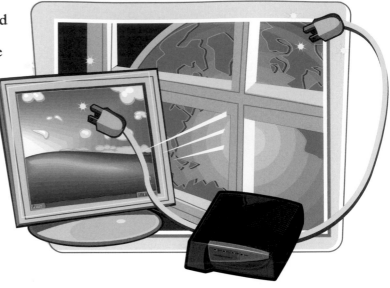

Cable Modems

Cable modems provide a high-speed Internet connection using the same cable line that brings the television signal into a building. Your local cable television provider supplies cable modems. Cable modems typically operate at least 10 times faster than a dial-up modem. Cable modems also provide *always-on* Internet access, meaning that you do not have to wait before using the Internet.

DSL Modems

Digital Subscriber Line (DSL) is a high-speed connection that your telephone company provides using your existing telephone line. The telephone company makes minor modifications to your existing phone line that allow you to send digital signals over the line along with your telephone signals without affecting the quality of your telephone calls. DSL, like cable modems, is usable while you are on the telephone and is *always-on* Internet access.

Connections

Traditional broadband modems connect to wireless equipment using a standard Ethernet network cable. Some broadband modems will only connect to a computer using a USB port. You cannot connect these modems directly to a wireless network. Newer broadband modems have built-in wireless and wired capabilities, which provide a single device that serves as your broadband modem, an Ethernet switch, and your wireless access point.

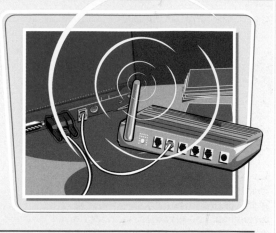

Number of Users

Some providers of high-speed connections that use broadband modems, such as cable or phone companies, may restrict you in the number of users that can use the connection. Always check with your connection provider to ensure that you can use the high-speed connection with a network, whether it is a wireless network or not.

Authentication

Broadband modems can use a variety of methods to authenticate a user before one can use the modem. Some broadband modems require connection to a computer with a specific name, while other modems use a name and password login. Wireless equipment that is attached to broadband modems can use these authentication methods.

Configure Network Bridges

You can use a network bridge to transfer data from one network to another regardless of whether one network is sending TCP/IP data while the other is sending NetBEUI data. *Network bridges* are simple devices that expand the coverage area of a wireless network, allowing two separate networks — even if the networks are different types and in different locations — to work as one.

You must configure the receiving computer to read the data it receives by setting up additional protocols. In addition, you must configure network interface cards to promiscuous mode; that is, the NIC listens to all traffic.

Ethernet Devices

A network bridge enables you to connect any Ethernet device to an existing wireless network quickly and easily. Some devices only have a built-in Ethernet port with no other means of connecting to a network, wireless or otherwise. A wireless bridge enables a device that would otherwise require an Ethernet cable to communicate with a wireless network.

Devices

Computers and laptops that are commonly connected to a wireless network can easily accept network interface devices such as wireless network adapters or PC card network adapters. You use wireless bridges to connect devices that have only a standard Ethernet port to a wireless network. Examples of devices that only have an Ethernet port are network printers, network storage devices, and even some computer gaming consoles.

Speed

As with all wireless devices, the speed at which information is transmitted depends on the standards that the device supports. Currently, two popular standards support transmission rates of 11 megabits per second (Mbps) and 54 Mpbs. Specialized wireless devices on the market today intended for use by large networks can operate as fast as 480 Mbps. Newer standards increase the speed to 3 gigabits per second (Gbps). The Ethernet port on the bridge allows a connection to any Ethernet device that uses a connection speed of up to 100 Mbps. Despite the speed at which the bridge communicates with the device, the device can only communicate with the wireless network at the maximum speed allowed by the bridge as it communicates with another wireless device on the network, such as a router.

Point to Point

It is possible to use two Ethernet wireless bridges to connect two devices or networks together without the use of other wireless devices, such as wireless routers. For example, you can use a network bridge connected to a network in an office to communicate with another network bridge connected to a network located in a warehouse on the other side of a road. This allows both networks to communicate with each other.

Web-Based Configuration

As with many wireless network devices, a network bridge's configuration is Web based. Regardless of the type of connection device to the bridge, you must connect the bridge to a computer, thereby enabling access to the configuration by using any Web browser.

Configure Residential Gateways

With a residential gateway, or *router*, you can quickly and easily connect multiple computers to the Internet using a high-speed Internet connection, such as a DSL or cable modem.

When you connect one computer to a high-speed Internet connection, you do not need a router. However, increasing the number of computers from one to many, you must install a router to manage all the network information between your computers and the broadband modem.

IP Address Allocation

All computers that access the Internet, whether connected wirelessly or not, must use a unique identifying number called an *IP address*. A residential router can automatically manage and assign IP numbers to computers connected to the same network to which the router belongs. The management of these IP numbers is accomplished using the *Dynamic Host Configuration Protocol*, more commonly called DHCP.

Configuration

The configuration of wireless routers is accomplished using any Web browser to access the configuration information of the router.

Security

Most residential routers now have built-in security features, such as data encryption, and additional software that increase the security of your network. Firewall applications that prevent unauthorized access to the router as well as information monitoring tools are now commonly available with many wireless routers. Some residential gateways even come with parental control software to help restrict access to objectionable content on the Internet.

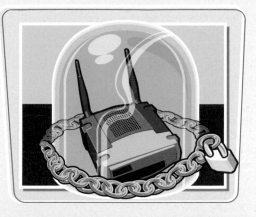

Ports

Most residential routers also have a built-in switch, or hub, that allows you to connect computers and other network devices, such as a network printer, directly to the router using standard Ethernet cables. Most routers have four built-in Ethernet ports. Regardless of the speed at which the router operates wirelessly, the built-in Ethernet ports can communicate with each other at speeds of up to 100 Mbps or even 1 Gbps.

Compatibility

All wireless residential routers can communicate with other devices that use the same communications protocol as the router. Most new routers support different transmission speeds, enabling you to use a wide range of wireless devices from many different manufacturers running at different transmission speeds.

Understanding Access Points

Access points provide network access for other wireless network devices. You can use access points to allow computers to share Internet connections, extend the reach of an existing wireless network, and provide connections to specific parts of a network, such as a printer bay or training room.

You can use the same type of wireless router you use for setting up a residential gateway as a wireless access point. In fact, many companies purchase the same router model to install as a gateway and access point.

Provide Access

The primary purpose of an access point is to provide an entry point to the network for other wireless devices. Any computer with a wireless adapter and within range of the access point can connect to the network.

Extend Coverage

You can use an access point to extend the coverage of a wireless network. For example, if a router is too far away from an area at the rear of a building, you can place an access point in the remote area to bring network access to any wireless devices there.

Limits

Depending on the number of users and the amount of network activity, some access points may have a limit on the number of users that can simultaneously use the network through the access point. Consult with the hardware manufacturer to determine the capabilities of the access point you set up.

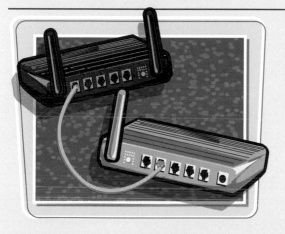

Ports

Unlike routers, some access points typically only have a single network port through which they connect to the network. You can connect the access point to an existing cable network via a hub or switch, or you can connect it to another wireless device, such as a wireless router.

Compatibility

As with all wireless network devices, make sure the access point can interoperate with the other wireless network devices on the network. Generally, devices from different manufacturers operate together as long as they use the same wireless standard.

Set Up a Wireless Gateway

You can connect computers to your wireless network after you set up your wireless gateway or *wireless router*, which links the internal wireless network with the Internet. You configure your gateway with a Web browser or setup program that your router supplies.

During set up, you may be asked for the IP address of the router. Sometimes your Internet service provider (ISP) gives this to you, but mostly your ISP assigns you an IP address. Depending on your ISP contract, you may need to periodically obtain a different IP address from your provider.

Set Up a Wireless Gateway

① In your Web browser, type
http://192.168.2.1 and press Enter.

Note: The default address of your gateway may be different; your gateway manual provides this information.

The Base Station Management Tool window appears.

② Type the administration password in the Password box.

③ Click **Log On**.

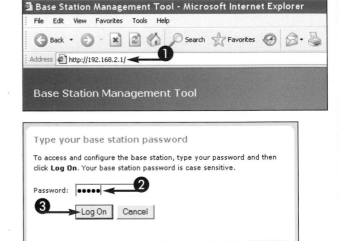

The window for viewing and renewing network information appears.

④ Click **Renew**.

Home
You can quickly and easily manage the Microsoft® Wireless Base Station. As you configure it, the base station's settings are displayed in the following tables.

Wide Area Network (WAN) Settings - Dynamic

This section displays a summary of Internet settings. The Internet is a wide area network. As you are troubleshooting problems with the base station, you can renew the base station's WAN IP address information. For information about releasing and renewing IP addresses, click **Help**.

Broadband connection: Connecting
WAN IP address:
Subnet mask:
Default gateway:
Primary Domain Name System (DNS):
Secondary DNS:

Release | Renew ④

Local Area Network (LAN) Settings

This section displays a summary of settings for your LAN.

Local IP address: 192.168.2.1
Subnet mask: 255.255.255.0
DHCP server: Enabled
Firewall: Enabled

DHCP Client List

This section lists the computers and other devices that the base station detects on your network.

● The IP address information from your ISP appears.

Note: Your ISP likely has assigned you a dynamic IP address. In some cases, such as if you are a business, your ISP assigns you a static, or permanent, IP address.

Home
You can quickly and easily manage the Microsoft® Wireless Base Station. As you configure it, the base station's settings are displayed in the following tables.

Wide Area Network (WAN) Settings - Dynamic

This section displays a summary of Internet settings. The Internet is a wide area network. As you are troubleshooting problems with the base station, you can renew the base station's WAN IP address information. For information about releasing and renewing IP addresses, click **Help**.

Broadband connection: Connect
WAN IP address: 192.168.2.1
Subnet mask: 255.255.255.0
Default gateway: 192.168.2.10
Primary Domain Name System (DNS):
Secondary DNS:

Release | Renew

TIPS

When should I change my security settings?
You should change the security settings of your wireless gateway after you set it up. However, do not enable encryption features on your hardware until your network is working. You can return and enable security features on your routers and computers later. To learn more about wireless network security, see Chapter 8.

How often do I have to obtain a new IP address?
Some providers have a 24-hour rule in which you must obtain a different IP address. Others may be longer. The acquisition and setup of these dynamic IP addresses are usually automatic.

Set Up an Access Point

You can set up additional wireless *access points*, or APs, to extend the range of your wireless network. You connect an AP to your wired network with an Ethernet cable and then configure the hardware with a Web browser.

To set up your access point, you must run the access point configuration utility. In most cases, this is a Web page that connects to your access point hardware (router). You can renew IP addresses, change time settings, upgrade the hardware's firmware, change passwords, and configure security settings.

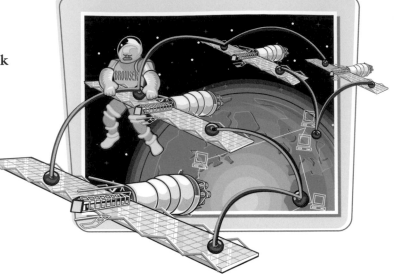

Set Up an Access Point

CHANGE THE PASSWORD

① To change the administration password, in your Web browser, type the address of your access point and press Enter.

② Click **Management**.

③ Click **Change Password**.

The access point home page appears.

The Change Password window appears.

④ Type your current password.

⑤ Type a new password.

⑥ Retype the password to confirm it.

⑦ Click **Apply**.

Your password is changed.

SET THE TIME ZONE

8 Click **Management**.

9 Click **Set Time**.

The Set Time window appears.

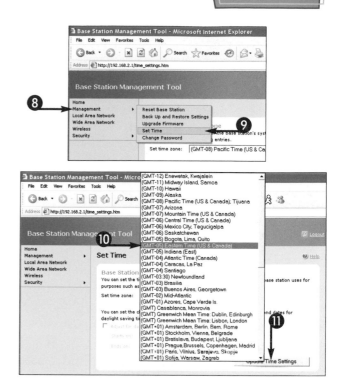

10 Click here and select a time zone.

11 Click **Update Time Settings**.

The time zone for your access point updates.

TIPS

What kind of wireless access points do manufacturers sell?

Manufacturers sell wireless access points that work with two or three different Wi-Fi modes. A dual-mode AP may work with the 802.11a and 802.11b technologies, while a tri-band AP may work with these modes plus the emerging 802.11g standard.

Should I set up security for an access point I use for my small business?

Yes, you should. Some access point hardware manufacturers now provide built-in encryption algorithms on their APs, although hackers have cracked some of these algorithms. Consider adding encryption to any data you send over a wireless network. Also, change all built-in passwords when you set up your AP hardware for the first time.

Download Firmware

You can download updates to the software, or *firmware*, that operates your router or other wireless access point. Firmware updates can improve the functionality of your hardware. Some firmware updates have bug fixes to common problems associated with your hardware, for example, to fix a bug that prevents more than four users from connecting to a router simultaneously.

Not all hardware requires or has firmware updates. However, as new operating systems and wireless standards emerge, manufacturers usually release firmware updates to keep their older hardware up to date.

Download Firmware

① In your Web browser, type the address of your access point and press Enter.

The access point home page appears.

② Click **Management**.

③ Click **Upgrade Firmware**.

The Upgrade Firmware window appears.

④ Click the **Microsoft Broadband Networking Web site** link.

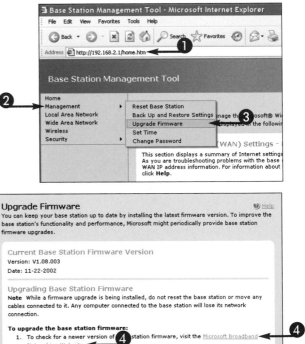

The Microsoft Broadband Networking page appears.

Note: *The link you click and visit depends on the manufacturer of your firmware.*

5 Click the **Update the firmware and software for your Microsoft Broadband networking devices** link.

A page that lets you download the firmware update appears.

6 Click the link for the latest firmware update.

Broadband Networking

- › Microsoft Help and Support
- › Microsoft's support LifeCycle for Broadband Networking products
- › Frequently asked questions regarding Microsoft's Support LifeCycle
- › Search the Microsoft Download Center for any available downloads
- **5** › Update the firmware and software for your Microsoft Broadband networking devices

---

Manual update

1. Download the MSBNDownload.exe firmware update. To do th   sit the following Microsoft Web site:
   http://go.microsoft.com/fwlink/?linkid=6790   **6**
2. Save the file to a location such as your desktop or the My Documents folder.
3. If you are updating a wireless base station, use an Ethernet cable to connect your computer to your base station.
4. To run the update, double-click the **MSBNDownload** file.
5. Follow the instructions that appear on the screen to update the firmware of your device.

While the firmware is being saved to your base station, the power light on the base station blinks and then turns orange.
completed. If the update fails, the power light continues to blink slowly until you successfully update the firmware. In this
again, or you can reset the base station.

↑ Back to the top

TIPS

Where should I store firmware updates?

You can save downloads to your desktop, where you can easily find them. You can delete a file after you update your hardware. You can create a directory called Downloads, or something similar, to store the software you download.

Will manufacturers keep me informed of updates?

Some manufactures do keep you informed after you register your product with them. Consider always registering the product as soon as you purchase it so you can get on the mailing list to receive update information. In fact, many times you cannot download the firmware updates without having an authorized user-name and password issued by the manufacturer.

continued

Download Firmware
(continued)

Before you actually download and install the firmware updates, read any release notes — information from the company about the updates — to see if any compatibility problems exist between your version of the hardware, your computer, and the new firmware updates. You may want to download and install the firmware update to a test machine before deploying it to multiple computers.

Firmware is available on most hardware manufacturer Web sites. Updating firmware reprograms an actual microchip in the router.

Download Firmware *(continued)*

The File Download – Security Warning dialog box appears.

7 Click **Save**.

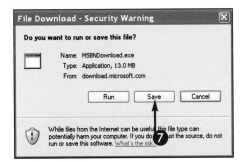

The Save As dialog box appears.

8 Select where you want to save the download.

9 Click **Save**.

A dialog box displays the progress of the download.

After the firmware downloads, you see the download Web page.

 You can follow the directions on this page to download the firmware you need.

4. On the **Management** menu, click **Back up and Restore Settings**.
5. Click **Back Up Settings**.
6. Click **Save**.
7. Type a name for the file that contains your base station settings or use the default name **Config.bin**.
8. Click the folder where you want to save the file, and then click **Save**.

Back to the top

Disable firewall or antivirus programs
For information about how to disable your firewall or antivirus programs, view the documentation that came with the program, or contact the manufacturer's technical support.

Back to the top

Install firmware update
Warning Do not install the firmware update from a computer that is connected to your base station by using a wireless network connection. If your wireless signal is interrupted, weakened, or interfered with while the firmware update is running, your base station may become unusable.

Automatic update
1. Start the Microsoft Broadband Network Utility.
2. On the **Help** menu, click **Check for Updates Online**. The Broadband Networking Update Service checks for updates by connecting to Microsoft. This can take several minutes, depending on your connection speed. If any new updates are available, a download screen appears. Otherwise, you receive a "No new updates are available" message.
3. Follow the instructions on the Broadband Networking Update Service page to update the firmware of your device.

If the automatic update fails, go to the "Manual Update" section.

Manual update
1. Download the **MSBNDownload.exe** firmware update. To do this, visit the following Microsoft Web site:
   http://go.microsoft.com/fwlink/?linkid=6790
2. Save the file to a location such as your desktop or the My Documents folder.
3. If you are updating a wireless base station, use an Ethernet cable to connect your computer to your base station.
4. To run the update, double-click the **MSBNDownload** file.
5. Follow the instructions that appear on the screen to update the firmware of your device.

While the firmware is being saved to your base station, the power light on the base station blinks and then turns orange. When the light is solid green, the update is completed. If the update fails, the power light continues to blink slowly until you successfully update the firmware. In this situation, you can try to update the firmware again, or you can reset the base station.

Back to the top

TIPS

Where can I find the Web site address for my fireware's manufacturer?

Manufacturers often print their Web site addresses on packaging or in instruction manuals. You also can use a search engine to locate the Web address for a manufacturer.

How long does it take to download the updates?

This depends on the product, connection speed, and how large the update file is. In most instances, the manufacturer updates the entire Setup program, which is usually several megabytes (MB) in size. With a dial-up connection, this may take 60 minutes or longer to download. For faster connections, this time is only a few minutes.

Upgrade Firmware

After downloading the latest version of firmware, you need to upgrade your hardware. Upgrading the firmware applies updates that may improve the performance of the device or increase the security.

In some cases, you can send your downloaded file to the hardware using a Web browser. In other cases, you need to upgrade the firmware by running a setup routine provided by the firmware update. Usually this setup routine is part of the file you download. You need to consult the manufacturer of your router to find out how to upgrade the firmware you use.

Upgrade Firmware

① In your Web browser, type the address of your access point and press Enter.

The access point home page appears.

② Click **Management**.

③ Click **Upgrade Firmware**.

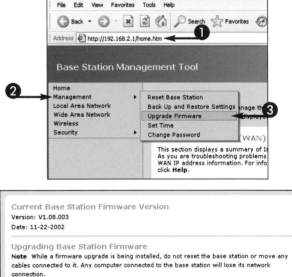

The Upgrade Firmware page appears.

④ Click **Browse**.

The Choose file dialog box appears.

⑤ Click the upgrade file.

⑥ Click **Open**.

● The file appears selected in the Web browser.

⑦ Click **Apply**.

A message asking if you are sure you want to continue appears.

⑧ Click **OK**.

The firmware upgrade completes.

When should I upgrade my fireware?

You are not required to upgrade firmware. In most cases, hardware runs well on the firmware version the manufacturer installs. However, new firmware versions you download from manufacturer Web sites may add new features to your hardware. Upgrading also can sometimes improve the speed and quality of your wireless network.

What happens if the update makes my network stop working?

Most updates include a utility to uninstall itself. In some cases, when you uninstall the update the original setup is automatically reinstalled for you. In other cases, you may need to uninstall the update, and then manually reinstall the original firmware software.

Introducing DHCP

Your wireless network router automatically assigns each of your computers a unique network address using *DHCP*, or *Dynamic Host Configuration Protocol*. DHCP makes it easier to add computers and other devices to your wireless network.

Microsoft Windows XP has built-in support for DHCP. When you first set up Windows, if you are already part of a network, you are prompted if you want to set up DHCP. If, however, you are not initially part of a network and you now want to attach to one that requires DHCP, you need to install and configure DHCP for your network.

IP Address

An *IP*, or *Internet Protocol*, address identifies your computer in a unique way, similar to how your postal mail address identifies where you live. An IP address is 32 bits long and looks like this: 208.215.179.146.

DHCP Server

Your wireless network gateway hardware probably has a built-in DHCP server. It assigns each computer on your network a dynamic IP address, either when a PC is turned on or when you manually request an IP address. In a computer-to-computer network, your host PC may act as a DHCP server, assigning IP addresses to client computers.

DHCP Clients

Your Windows XP computers are configured by default to automatically request an IP address from a DHCP server. In some cases, such as when setting up a host computer for a computer-to-computer network, you should turn off this automatic feature and assign your computer a permanent, or static, IP address. A static IP address is one that is permanently assigned to your computer. It does not change, even if you connect to a different wireless network. In cases in which you access multiple networks, you may need to re-enable DHCP for those networks that have the DHCP server.

Network Address Translation

Your router likely has built-in Network Address Translation (NAT) support. NAT is an Internet standard that provides your internal network with its own set of IP addresses, usually beginning with 192.168.1.1, which does not conflict with Internet addresses. NAT also hides your computers so Internet users cannot see them from outside your network. Depending on the router and its configuration settings, NAT tables can become outdated and not include the most current addressing information. Administrators can force the router to update the NAT when several new computers join the network.

Installing Wireless Hardware in PCs

Your computer communicates with your wireless network using a network adapter. You can install an internal or external adapter, depending on whether your computer is a desktop or laptop PC. When you shop for wireless equipment, consider the type of wireless networking card to use in your computer. Wireless network cards may or may not have a small antenna attached to it, depending on whether you use them on a desktop or a laptop.

Discover Wireless Adapters

To communicate with a wireless network, you may need to install hardware in your computer. Some computers require two or more network adapters to communicate with multiple networks.

As long as the computer has connections for the adapters, there is no restriction on the number of network adapters that you can attach or Pickup into a computer. You can also use wireless network adapters in the same computer that has standard Ethernet cable network adapters.

Software Drivers

The wireless network adapter includes software that you must install before you Pickup the wireless card. You may even have to install the software before installing the hardware. The software contains device drivers to enable the network card to communicate with the operating system. Some operating systems may already have the necessary drivers built in, and the installation of software is not necessary. Consult you network card's documentation for more information.

Antenna

Most wireless adapters have an antenna attached for transmitting and receiving signals from other wireless network devices. The antenna is attached to the network card and placed at the rear of the computer. Position the computer and leave enough clearance to install and move the antenna, because moving the antenna may increase the signal quality.

Lights

Most network adapters, including wireless network adapters, have a number of lights on the adapter that you can use to provide information about the status of the adapter. A power light indicates that the adapter is receiving power. A connection light may indicate the network adapter has detected and connected to a wireless network. When initially testing your wireless network adapter, you should position your computer and adapter so that you can view the lights on the wireless network adapter.

Warranty

All computer hardware that you install in your computer should come with a warranty. The validity of the warranty of the hardware, and even the computer, may depend on you following the correct installation process for your card. For example, some computer manufacturers may void your warranty if you install your own hardware. Always refer to the warranty specifications for your computer and your new hardware for details on any steps you must take to avoid invalidating the warranty.

Wireless Network Kits

Some manufacturers now sell all the necessary hardware to create a wireless network in a complete kit. The kit usually consists of one or two network adapters and a wireless network router. When purchasing a wireless network kit, you must ensure that the network adapter in the kit is suitable for use with your computer.

Using Wireless Adapters

Each computer on your wireless network requires a wireless network adapter. Your network adapter acts as a radio transceiver, sending and receiving data across your wireless network. You can choose from several types of network adapters, which are also called *network interface cards*, or *NICs*.

You must connect a NIC either to or inside your computer. Some NICs require you to open the case of your computer and install the device internally. Others connect to one of your USB (Universal Serial Bus) ports from the outside. Another type slides into a laptop computer's PC card slot. For some small handheld devices, you use CompactFlash wireless adapters.

PCI Adapter

Most computers have expansion slots inside the computer that allow you to add functionality to a computer. You can install a network adapter in a *PCI*, or *Peripheral Component Interconnect*, slot inside your desktop computer. PCI slots are the most common type of expansion slots in a computer. You need to open the computer case, find an empty PCI slot, and then install the adapter.

PC Card Adapter

You can install a *PC card-compatible network adapter* in your laptop computer. A PC card is a small credit-card-sized adapter that fits into most laptop computers, adding functionality to the laptop.

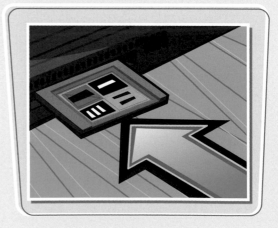

USB Adapter

A *USB network adapter* plugs into a USB slot, which is available on both desktop and laptop computers. USB adapters are quick and easy to install. You do not have to open the computer to install them, and in many cases, the operating system automatically configures the USB.

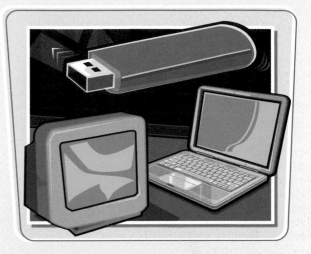

CompactFlash Adapter

Handheld computers are very small computers that perform a wide variety of information management tasks, such as tracking expenses, recording contact information, and scheduling meetings. Many handheld computers can connect to a wireless network using a *CompactFlash wireless adapter card*. Once connected to the wireless network, you can exchange information between the handheld computer and other computers on the network. CompactFlash adapters incorporate security technology to provide 64- and 128-bit encryption to help ensure your data is secure as you access wireless networks. Some CompactFlash adapters also include a port for wired network connections, making it possible for your handheld device to connect to conventional wired networks. CompactFlash adapters are easy to use because all you do is slide them into your device and let your device configure them. Finally, these adapters do not require a separate power source to run them.

Install and Configure a Network Adapter

You can install a PCI-compatible network adapter in a desktop computer or a PC card-compatible network adapter in a laptop or notebook computer so your computer can communicate with your wireless network.

Installation steps depend on the adapter. Although the actual steps may vary, in most cases you use wizards, so the steps in this section are similar to what you see. Consult your network card instructions for specific procedures.

INSTALL A NETWORK ADAPTER

❶ Pickup the installation CD-ROM.

The wireless adapter installation screen appears.

❷ Click **Next** to continue.

The Before continuing with Setup screen appears.

❸ Click **Next**.

The End-User License Agreement screen appears.

The End-User License Agreement screen appears.

4 Click the **I Agree** option (○ changes to ◉).

5 Click Next.

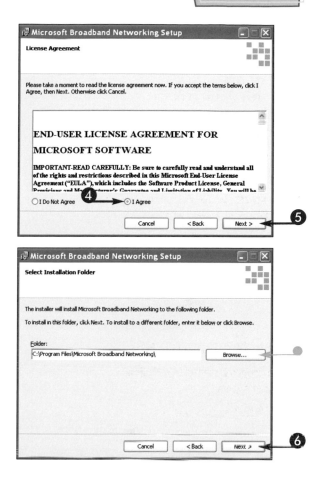

The Select Installation Folder screen appears.

● You can click Browse to select a different folder to place the installment.

6 Click **Next**.

TIPS

Do I need the latest update to the software before I install my adapter?

In most cases you can install the software on the CD-ROM and then upgrade it to the latest version from the manufacturer's Web site after your wireless network is up and running.

What are the ways network adapters connect to computers?

Typically, you install a network adapter in a PCI, or Peripheral Component Interconnect, by opening the computer case, finding an empty PCI slot, and then installing the adapter. To install a PC card in your notebook, you simply slide the card into the side of your laptop computer.

You can configure your wireless network adapter with custom software that many manufacturers supply with their hardware. Some of the provided utilities enable you to modify configuration settings, such as speed and protocol settings. Others let you monitor and log adapter performance. With the monitoring and logging capabilities, you can track and troubleshoot problems that may arise with your network adapter.

You should disable Automatic Wireless Network Configuration if you are installing and using configuration utility software. The network adapter utility that installs with your network adapter may be different from the one shown here.

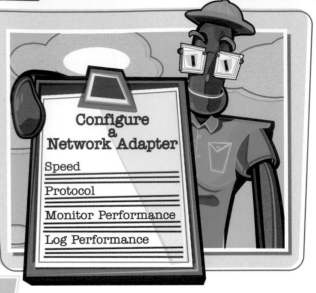

Install and Configure a Network Adapter *(continued)*

The Software Installation is Complete screen appears.

⑦ Click **Next** to finish.

⑧ Plug in the USB wireless adapter to a USB port on your computer.

● A **Wireless Network Connection** icon (🖳) appears on the taskbar.

USING NETWORK ADAPTER UTILITIES

1 Double-click the **Broadband Network Utility** icon (🖳) on the taskbar.

*Note: Windows XP may warn you that the software has not passed Windows logo testing; if so, click **Continue**.*

The Microsoft Broadband Network Utility dialog box appears.

● You can view the signal strength.

● You can view the connection speed.

● You can view the IP address.

● You can view file and printer sharing status.

 TIPS

I see a warning logo when I install a new device. What does this mean?

Microsoft tests many devices that will work with Windows. Devices that Microsoft has not certified generate the logo warning error when you install them. Many devices that generate the logo warning were created after Windows was last updated, or they are new and may be certified in the future.

Where can I learn more about new devices?

You can click the Learn about accessing files on these devices link on the Microsoft Broadband Network Utility dialog box to learn more about wireless networking features and capabilities.

Confirm Driver Installation

You can confirm the successful installation of your network adapter in Windows XP Device Manager. You can also reinstall the software driver for your hardware if Device Manager does not list your network adapter.

The Device Manager is helpful when you are experiencing problems with your wireless networking connection because you can easily see the hardware devices installed on your computer and the status of the hardware – working or not working. The Device Manager also enables you to remove a hardware device or reinstall a device that may not be working correctly.

Confirm Driver Installation

1 Click **start**.

2 Click **Control Panel**.

The Control Panel appears.

3 Click **Performance and Maintenance**.

The Performance and Maintenance window appears.

④ Click the **System** icon ().

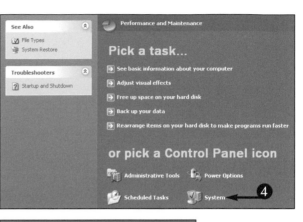

The System Properties dialog box appears.

⑤ Click the **Hardware** tab.

continued

Sometimes I lose network connections. Is this a problem with the hardware?

You may need to confirm driver installation if you are experiencing difficulty with your network hardware. Incorrect driver installation can cause many different types of problems with network adapters.

At work, why is the Device Manager not showing up?

Your system administrator has removed the Device Manager from your user profile. This prevents you from changing settings or disabling a hardware device without the system administrator's authorization. Consult your system administrator for more information.

Many manufacturers regularly update and release new software drivers for your hardware, providing new features and better stability. You can download these updates and install them on your computer. As with any device, your new network adapter may attempt to use resources already allocated to another device in the computer.

Check your operating system's documentation to resolve resource conflicts, or to temporarily remove any unnecessary hardware, such as a sound card, until you configure the wireless network adapter and have it working. If the network adapter appears correctly installed, but you cannot communicate with an existing network, double-check the network adapter settings.

Confirm Driver Installation *(continued)*

6 Click **Device Manager**.

The Device Manager window appears.

7 Click the plus sign (⊞) beside Network adapters.

A list of network adapters appears.

● The icon ( ) beside the wireless PC card shows the driver is installed and the adapter is working.

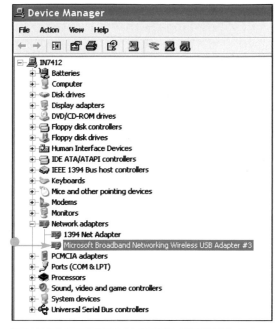

● The red X through the icon ( ) shows the network adapter is not working properly.

TIPS

How do I uninstall or disable a network adapter?

To uninstall or disable a network adapter driver, right-click a network adapter in the Device Manager. Click **Disable** or **Uninstall**. Your computer disables or uninstalls the network adapter driver.

My network adapter worked fine yesterday, but does not today. What should I do?

One of the easiest fixes is to shut down Windows and then restart your computer. This forces Windows to look for all your hardware, including the network adapter, when it boots. Many times this gets your network adapter back.

Update Adapter Firmware

Most network adapter manufacturers provide updates to their hardware. Periodically, you may want to visit your adapter manufacturer's Web site to find any available updates, especially when you encounter problems. Some manufacturers also include forms you can fill out to receive e-mails or other types of correspondence alerting you to new updates and releases.

Finally, after you download any updates to your firmware, you must install them on your computer. This activates them for your wireless network adapter.

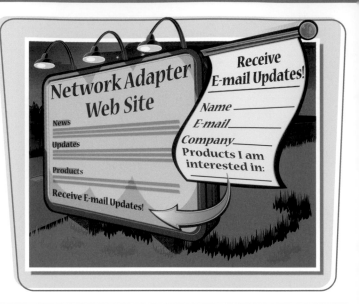

Update Adapter Firmware

① In your Web browser, type **http://support. microsoft.com/kb/814445** and press Enter.

Note: If your hardware is made by a different manufacturer, type the Web address of the manufacturer that makes your hardware.

The Microsoft page for updating the adapter firmware appears.

② Click the filename.

Install firmware update

Warning Do not install the firmware update from a computer that is connected to your base station by using a wireless n
interrupted, weakened, or interfered with while the firmware update is running, your base station may become unusable.

Automatic update

1. Start the Microsoft Broadband Network Utility.

2. On the **Help** menu, click **Check for Updates Online**. The Broadband Networking Update Service checks for update
several minutes, depending on your connection speed. If any new updates are available, a download screen appears
updates are available" message.

3. Follow the instructions on the Broadband Networking Update Service page to update the firmware of your device.

If the automatic update fails, go to the "Manual Update" section.

Manual update

1. Download the MSBNDownload.exe firmware update. To do th[?] [?]it the following Microsoft Web site:

    http://go.microsoft.com/fwlink/?linkid=6790

2. Save the file to a location such as your desktop or the My Documents folder.

3. If you are updating a wireless base station, use an Ethernet cable to connect your computer to your base station.

4. To run the update, double-click the **MSBNDownload** file.

5. Follow the instructions that appear on the screen to update the firmware of your device.

While the firmware is being saved to your base station, the power light on the base station blinks and then turns orange. W
completed. If the update fails, the power light continues to blink slowly until you successfully update the firmware. In this s
again, or you can reset the base station.

The File Download – Security Warning dialog box appears.

3 Click **Save**.

The Save As dialog box appears.

4 Click here and select where you want to save the download.

5 Click **Save**.

Firmware downloads to your computer.

TIPS

What do I do after I download the firmware software?

After you download the firmware update to your computer, locate the file using My Computer or Windows Explorer and double-click the file. This activates the setup program, which then walks you through installing the update on your computer.

Do I have to shut down and restart Windows after I update my firmware?

Usually the update installation program asks you to shut down and restart Windows. If it does not direct you to and your network adapter is not working properly after the update, go ahead and shut down and restart Windows.

Configuring Wireless Networks

After you install a wireless network adapter in your computer, you can configure your wireless networks and view how well they are working as this chapter shows you. Although Windows XP computers using wireless technologies can connect to multiple wireless networks, they can only connect to one network at a time. If you use a particular wireless network, make sure that you specify the correct settings — called the service set identifier (SSID) — of the network you want to connect to, otherwise Windows XP may connect to another wireless network instead.

View Available Networks

You can automatically configure your wireless network adapter to view available networks. This feature saves you time because you do not have to manually configure your wireless network. When you turn on your computer with an installed wireless network adapter, Windows searches the area for wireless signals, picking up radio and infrared signals from your surroundings, and displaying a list of available networks.

A nice feature of Windows XP is the taskbar messages that display when it finds a network. In the lower right corner of the taskbar by the clock, a small window appears when an available network is found.

View Available Networks

① Right-click the **Network Connection** icon (▣).

② Click **View Available Wireless Networks**.

The Wireless Network Connection dialog box appears.

③ Click the network to which you want to connect.

④ Click **Connect**.

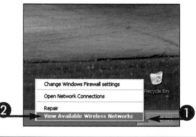

● The Connect button changes to the Disconnect button after your computer connects to the wireless network.

⑤ Click the **Close** button to exit from the Wireless Network Connection dialog box.

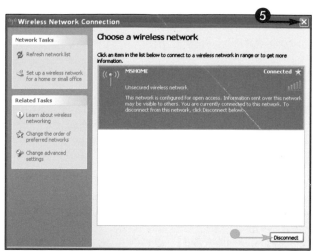

● A text balloon appears, showing the speed and signal strength of your wireless network.

Note: For more about network speed and signal strength, see the section "View Signal Strength."

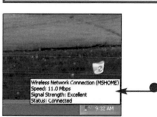

TIPS

Why does the Wireless Network Connection dialog box show more networks than just mine?

The Wireless Network Connection dialog box displays all wireless networks within reception range of your computer. If it displays more than one network, either there are multiple wireless networks available in your home or office, or you are picking up signals from an open network operating in a neighboring business or residence.

What if a network in my area is not showing up?

There are several reasons. One problem may be that the network may use different protocols from what you have set up on your computer. Another problem may be with the network hardware, the access point hardware, for example. Consider shutting down and restarting the network hardware to see if it becomes available.

Configure an Available Network

Even with the automatic configuration of wireless networks, some wireless networks may not appear in the list Windows finds. Most wireless networks used by businesses, schools, and hospitals require you to configure a network connection manually to help keep out unauthorized users. In these cases, you must manually configure the network.

You can configure an available wireless network. Your computer saves your settings and adds the network to the Preferred networks list. To make changes to configure a network, you must log on using an administrator's account.

Configure an Available Network

① From the Wireless Network Connection dialog box, click **Change advanced settings**.

Note: To access the Wireless Network Connection dialog box, see the section "View Available Networks."

Note: You must have administrator privileges on your computer to configure settings in the Wireless Network Connection dialog box.

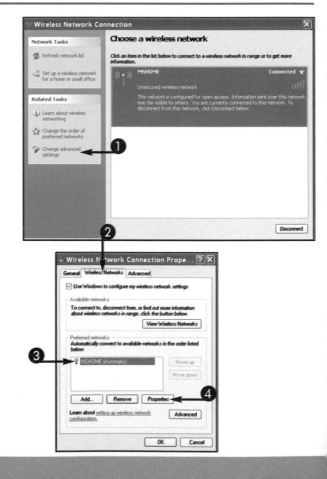

The Wireless Network Connection Properties dialog box appears.

② Click the **Wireless Networks** tab.

③ Select a network from the Preferred networks list.

④ Click **Properties**.

The properties dialog box for the network you selected appears.

⑤ Click here and select **Shared** if the network uses a network key for authentication.

⑥ Click **OK**.

Windows configures the available network to use the Shared network key property.

⑦ Click **OK** in the Wireless Network Connection Properties dialog box.

Your network is configured.

TIPS

How do I update the list of networks?

You can manually update the list of available networks. To do this, on the **Wireless Networks** tab of the Wireless Network Connection Properties dialog box, click **Refresh** in the Available networks area.

How do I change settings in the Wireless Network Connection dialog box if I do not have administrator privileges?

You cannot. You must ask your system administrator to grant you administrator privileges. If you are not authorized to have these privileges, you cannot make changes to your setting. If, however, you are configuring a home computer, log in as the administrator and you will have those privileges.

Add a Preferred Network

You can add a preferred network to your list of available networks so that Windows XP automatically connects to it. Windows attempts to connect to a *preferred network* each time you turn on your computer and you have an installed wireless network adapter. If a Preferred wireless network is not available or out of range, Windows shows you that it is unavailable.

To add a network to the preferred list, you need to know the name of the network – its SSID, or service set identifier – and if it requires a network key to connect to it.

Add a Preferred Network

① From the Wireless Network Connection Properties dialog box, click **Add**.

Note: To access the Wireless Network Connection dialog box, see the section "View Available Networks."

The Wireless network properties dialog box appears.

② Type the name of your wireless network in the Network name (SSID) field.

Note: To learn more about SSIDs, see Chapter 8.

❸ Click **OK**.

Wireless network properties
Association | Authentication | Connection

Network name (SSID): CorpNet

Wireless network key

This network requires a key for the following:

Network Authentication: Open
Data encryption: WEP

Network key:
Confirm network key:

Key index (advanced): 1
☑ The key is provided for me automatically

☐ This is a computer-to-computer (ad hoc) network; wireless access points are not used

❸ → OK | Cancel

● Windows XP adds the network to the Preferred networks list.

Wireless Network Connection Prope...
General | Wireless Networks | Advanced

☑ Use Windows to configure my wireless network settings

Available networks:
To connect to, disconnect from, or find out more information about wireless networks in range, click the button below.
View Wireless Networks

Preferred networks:
Automatically connect to available networks in the order listed below.

CorpNet (Automatic) | Move up
MSHOME (Automatic) | Move down

Add... | Remove | Properties

Learn about setting up wireless network configuration. | Advanced

OK | Cancel

TIPS

My network requires a key setting. How do I configure these?

You can configure the Wireless network key settings in the **Association** tab of the Wireless network properties dialog box. These settings must match the network key settings of the network you are adding. To learn about wireless network security, see Chapter 8.

Can I have two preferred networks — one for work and one for home?

No. Windows lets you set up just one as the preferred network, which it will try to find first. If it cannot find the preferred network, Windows attempts to find the next network in the list.

Remove a Preferred Network

You can remove a wireless network from the Preferred networks list when you no longer need to frequently connect to it. You may do this after you leave an area with a public wireless network that you plan not to visit again. Or you may no longer need to access a company-wide wireless network using your personal laptop.

By removing the network from the list, Windows XP stops looking for this network when you start your computer and decreases your boot time, because Windows no longer searches for (and connects to if it is found) a wireless network you do not want to access.

Remove a Preferred Network

① From the Wireless Network Connection Properties dialog box, click a preferred network.

Note: To access the Wireless Network Connection dialog box, see the section "View Available Networks."

② Click **Remove**.

Windows removes the preferred network.

Move a Preferred Network

You can rearrange available networks in the Preferred networks list. Because Windows XP uses the list to determine the order in which it connects to your preferred networks, you move a network to the bottom of the list if you know one network is not available in your area. Windows finds another network first and does not search for the unavailable network.

Also, you may want to place a preferred network at the top of the list if you know it is the one you most frequently want to log on to, but you want to keep other wireless networks listed for future usage. You do not need to reconfigure the other networks even though you use them less frequently than your main network.

Move a Preferred Network

① From the Wireless Network Connection Properties dialog box, click a preferred network.

Note: To access the Wireless Network Connection dialog box, see the section "View Available Networks."

② Click **Move up**.

● You can click **Move down** to move a network lower on the list.

● The preferred network moves higher on the Preferred networks list.

View Signal Strength

You can view a signal strength meter in Windows XP that displays the strength of the radio waves your computer receives from your wireless network. The signal strength meter helps you determine if you are within range of your wireless network, and how fast information is moving across your network.

The strength of a wireless network signal depends on several factors. Among these factors are the distance from the wireless network, the placement of your computer next to other devices that can interfere with signals, and your computer's battery life.

View Signal Strength

① Double-click the **Network Connection** icon (🖳).

The Wireless Network Connection Status dialog box appears.

● The status of your wireless network connection appears.

● The name of the network to which you are connected appears.

● The duration of your wireless network connection appears.

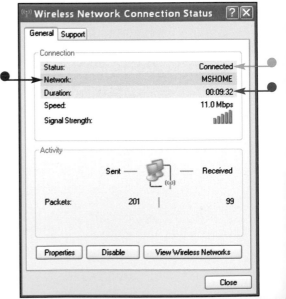

● The speed of your wireless network connection displays in megabits per second (Mbps).

● The signal strength of your wireless network connection appears here.

Note: You should move your access point or your computer until you reach a signal strength of 4 or 5.

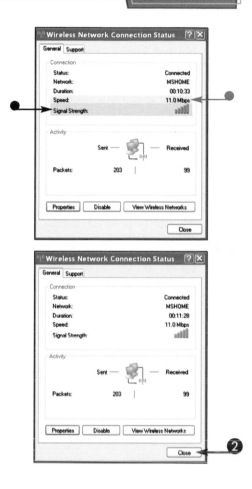

② Click **Close**.

The Wireless Network Connection Status dialog box closes.

 TIPS

Is there a quicker way to see the signal strength?

Yes. There are other ways you can view signal strength. You can position your mouse pointer over the **Network Connection** icon ( ) in your taskbar notification area. A text balloon appears, displaying network signal strength and speed. You also can view your signal strength with software utilities made by your hardware manufacturer.

What should my signal strength setting read?

A signal strength of 11 Mbps (megabits per second) is a standard to use. If your network card is connecting at a speed far lower than this, consider purchasing a new network card or contacting your network card manufacturer. Your card may not be configured properly to achieve maximum results.

Windows XP helps you quickly create a wireless network with the Wireless Zero Configuration feature. When you confirm that the Wireless Zero Configuration feature is on, you can avoid problems when you install and configure your hardware.

Usually, Windows XP automatically turns on the Zero Configuration service when you install a wireless networking device, such as a wireless network interface adapter. However, there are times when Windows XP does not automatically enable the service or when another device disables the service. In either case, you should enable it to help you configure your wireless network connection.

Confirm Zero Configuration Is On

① Click **start**.

② Click **Control Panel**.

The Control Panel window appears.

③ Click **Performance and Maintenance**.

The Performance and Maintenance window appears.

④ Click the **Administrative Tools** icon (📁).

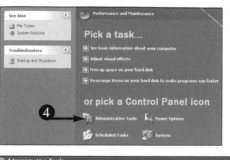

The Administrative Tools window appears.

TIPS

What do I do if Windows fails to configure my interface card?

You can set up a wireless network interface card if Windows XP fails to configure it automatically. First, confirm that the Windows XP Wireless Zero Configuration feature is enabled. To confirm zero configuration is on, perform Steps 1 to 7. If this feature is enabled but Windows XP does not configure your hardware, you can install configuration software that most manufacturers include with their network adapters.

Can I disable Zero Configuration?

Yes, but you may not be able to access the Internet via the wireless network. Some hardware manufacturers require Zero Configuration to be turned on for Internet connectivity to work.

continued

Confirm Zero Configuration Is On *(continued)*

You can use Automatic Wireless Network Configuration with newer wireless network interface cards that Microsoft certifies as working with Windows XP. Some older wireless network interface cards (NICs) may have updated software drivers you can download from the NIC manufacturer's Web site.

You need administrator privileges to turn Wireless Zero Configuration on or off. If you do not have administrator privileges, contact your system administrator or IT (information technology) department to ask how you can start the Wireless Zero Configuration service on your computer.

Confirm Zero Configuration Is On *(continued)*

5 Double-click the **Services** icon ().

The Services window appears.

6 Scroll down to the bottom of the window.

7 Click **Wireless Zero Configuration**.

8 Click the **Start the service** link.

Note: If the Stop the service link appears instead of the Start the service link, your computer is already running the Wireless Zero Configuration service.

● The Wireless Zero Configuration service starts.

Uninterruptible Power Supply	Manages a...		Manual	Local Service
Universal Plug and Play Device Host	Provides s...		Manual	Local Service
Volume Shadow Copy	Manages a...		Manual	Local System
WebClient	Enables Wi...	Started	Automatic	Local Service
Windows Audio	Manages a...	Started	Automatic	Local System
Windows Firewall/Internet Connection Sha...	Provides n...	Started	Automatic	Local System
Windows Image Acquisition (WIA)	Provides im...	Sta...	Automatic	Local System
Windows Installer	Adds, modi...		Manual	Local System
Windows Management Instrumentation	Provides a...	Started	Automatic	Local System
Windows Time	Maintains d...	Started	Automatic	Local System
Windows User Mode Driver Framework	Enables Wi...	Sta...ed	Automatic	Local Service
Wireless Zero Configuration	Provides a...	Started	Automatic	Local System
WMI Performance Adapter	Provides p...		Manual	Local System
Workstation	Creates an...	Started	Automatic	Local System

9 Click the **Close** icon (X).

The Services window closes.

Name	Description	Status	Startup Type	Log On As
Remote Procedure Call (RPC)	Provides th...	Started	Automatic	Network S...
Remote Procedure Call (RPC) Locator	Manages t...		Manual	Network S...
Removable Storage			Manual	Local System
Routing and Remote Access	Offers rout...		Disabled	Local System
Secondary Logon	Enables st...	Started	Automatic	Local System
Security Accounts Manager	Stores sec...	Started	Automatic	Local System
Security Center	Monitors s...	Started	Automatic	Local System
Server	Supports fil...	Started	Automatic	Local System
Shell Hardware Detection	Provides n...	Started	Automatic	Local System
Smart Card	Manages a...		Manual	Local Service
SSDP Discovery Service	Enables dis...	Started	Manual	Local Service

TIPS

How do I troubleshoot the Wireless Zero Configuration service?
If the service is already running, you can restart the Wireless Zero Configuration service. This may be helpful when you need to troubleshoot your wireless network. To restart the service, perform Steps **1** to **7**. In Step **8**, click **Restart the service**.

What version of Windows XP do I need for this service?
To get the Wireless Zero Configuration service, you must have Windows XP, Service Pack 2 (SP2). If you do not have this service pack, visit the Windows XP Service Pack 2 Web site at www.microsoft.com/windowsxp/sp2/default.mspx to learn more about it. You can download SP2 from that site as well.

Disable and Enable Automatic Configuration

Automatic Wireless Network Configuration automatically configures your wireless network adapter and connects you to your wireless network. You can disable the Automatic Wireless Network Configuration feature in Windows XP when you need to install software updates that the manufacturers provide with their network interface cards.

After you install software updates, you need to enable the Automatic Wireless Network Configuration to let Windows automatically configure your wireless network adapter each time you boot your computer. If the Automatic Wireless Network Configuration feature is disabled, the next time you restart Windows it may reenable automatically. If it does not, you have to reenable it manually using the steps here.

Disable and Enable Automatic Configuration

DISABLE AUTOMATIC CONFIGURATION

 From the Wireless Network Connection dialog box, click to deselect the **Use Windows to configure my wireless network settings** option (☑ changes to ☐).

***Note:** To access the Wireless Network Connection dialog box, see the section "View Available Networks."*

② Click **OK**.

Windows disables the automatic configuration of your wireless network settings.

ENABLE AUTOMATIC CONFIGURATION

1 From the Wireless Network Connection dialog box, click the **Use Windows to configure my wireless network settings** option (☐ changes to ☑).

Note: To access the Wireless Network Connection dialog box, see the section "View Available Networks."

2 Click **OK**.

Windows enables the automatic configuration of your wireless network settings.

TIPS

Should I keep the automatic configuration feature turned on if I have a laptop computer?

Yes. When using a laptop or portable computer, you should keep automatic configuration turned on as a default. This way Windows will be able to connect to and configure your wireless network settings when you enter an area that has a wireless network available.

I get an error that says "Error: server could not be found". What should I do?

Re-enable the Wireless Zero Configuration service. This allows you to access the Internet again.

Create a Wireless Bridge

You can connect, or *bridge*, one network with another network. For example, you can bridge an Ethernet-wired network with your wireless network. A network bridge lets you connect your laptop computer to your home or office network without requiring an additional wireless access point.

Another place where you might see a wireless network bridge is with gaming console setups. You can use a bridge to connect your game console – a Microsoft Xbox, for example – to your wireless network and other computers.

Create a Wireless Bridge

① Right-click .

② Click **Open Network Connections**.

The Network Connections window appears, displaying enabled connections.

③ Click the network connections you want to bridge.

To select multiple network connections, you can press and hold **Ctrl** and then click your selections.

Note: You cannot bridge network connections that have Internet Connection Sharing or Internet Connection Firewall enabled.

④ Right-click your selected network connections.

⑤ Click **Bridge Connections**.

● Windows bridges your network connections.

TIPS

Do I need to do anything different if my computer bridges two networks?

A computer that is bridging two or more networks needs at least two network adapters. In the case of an Ethernet-wired network and a wireless network, your computer needs an Ethernet adapter and a wireless network adapter.

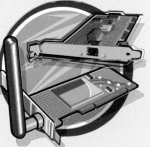

Is a server computer a better choice for a bridge?

If you plan to have more than ten users on your network using your computer as a bridge, consider investing in a dedicated server computer for this task. Your computer will not have to service the network requests then, leaving more processing capabilities for your normal work.

Creating Computer-to-Computer Networks

Computers can communicate directly with each other through a computer-to-computer network. In this chapter, you learn how to create a computer-to-computer network and share an Internet connection. This network is less expensive to set up than an infrastructure network because there are fewer pieces of equipment, such as routers, to purchase.

Understanding Computer-to-Computer Considerations

Many issues can help you decide if you should use a computer-to-computer network, or a more centralized network setup. Some of these include overall cost of the network, features of the operating systems, how well the computers communicate with each other, the distance between the computers, and the practical size of the network.

Cost

Connecting computers together in a computer-to-computer network requires each computer to have a wireless network adapter. Items, such as a wireless router or an access point, are not required. This makes a computer-to-computer network less expensive to set up than a more centralized network.

Operating Systems

Most modern operating systems have enough network functionality built into them so that you can use network features between just two computers. Usernames, passwords, and file and print sharing are available on almost all operating systems, allowing you to take full advantage of the services and resources of all computers in the network.

Compatibility

As long as the wireless adapters in each computer use the same network standard, the network adapters can communicate with each other regardless of the type or manufacturer of the wireless adapter. Internal wireless adapters installed inside a computer can communicate with other internal and external wireless adapters that you may attach to a computer USB port.

Size

There is no practical limit to the number of computers that can communicate in a computer-to-computer network. As long as each computer has a wireless adapter and is in range of all the other computers in the network, they work on the network. In practice, if your network has more than five computers, you may want to consider using a more centralized network layout using a wireless switch or other type of wireless access point.

Range

The distance between computers on a computer-to-computer network depends solely on the coverage area of the network adapters. You must have all network computers in range of each other for the network to work effectively. This means you can reduce the geographic size of the network when using a network adapter with a reduced range.

Computer-to-Computer versus Infrastructure Networks

Each network type has its own benefits and disadvantages. Before setting up a larger and more costly infrastructure network, consider setting up a computer-to-computer network first. Then try out the capabilities of the network. If the capabilities and performance of this type of network are all you need, keep it.

However, if you need a network that requires centralized management, advanced network security, and backup resources for the network, then consider a larger, infrastructure network.

Infrastructure Network Ratings

	−	+
Set Up Speed		
Extra Equipment		
Easy to Change		
Redundancy		
Mobile		

VS

Computer-to-Computer Network Ratings

	−	+
Set Up Speed		
Extra Equipment		
Easy to Change		
Redundancy		
Mobile		

Setup Speed

The time you need to set up a computer-to-computer network is significantly less than setting up an infrastructure network because less hardware is required. Once you install the wireless adapter in a computer and configure it, the network is operational and ready for use.

Extra Equipment

Complexity and costs are reduced in a computer-to-computer network because you use fewer hardware devices. Administration is also easy to manage because each user is responsible for his or her own computer, and administrators are not required for devices, such as routers and access points.

Easy to Change

Because a computer-to-computer network is not a fixed collection of wireless devices, you can add or remove wireless nodes as necessary.

Redundancy

In computer-to-computer networks, multiple wireless devices communicate with each other. If one wireless device is no longer available, a computer can still communicate with the network by communicating with other devices in range. On an infrastructure network, if a single device, such as an access point fails, many users can be disconnected from the network.

Mobile

Computer-to-computer networks are easy to move because the wireless devices are not permanent like wireless hubs. It is even possible to operate a computer-to-computer network between mobile computers located in moving vehicles.

Configure Host PCs

You create a computer-to-computer wireless network with Internet access by connecting a second or third computer to a PC that has an Internet connection. You must configure one computer as the host PC.

The host PC is the "main" computer on the network for other client PCs to connect to. The host computer connects directly to the Internet connection, and then client computers connect through the host to the Internet.

① Double-click the Network Connection icon (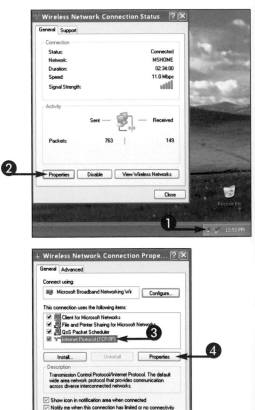).

The Wireless Network Connection Status dialog box appears.

② Click Properties.

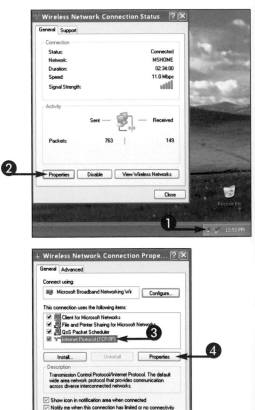

The Wireless Network Connection Properties dialog box appears.

③ Click the Internet Protocol (TCP/IP) option (☐ changes to ☑).

④ Click Properties.

The Internet Protocol (TCP/IP) Properties dialog box appears.

5 Click the **Use the following IP address** option (○ changes to ◉).

6 Type **192.168.0.1**.

7 Press Tab.

● Windows automatically fills in your subnet mask.

8 Click **OK**.

The Internet Protocol (TCP/IP) Properties dialog box closes.

9 Click the **Wireless Networks** tab.

10 Click **Advanced**.

continued

TIPS

What are peer-to-peer networks?

Computer-to-computer wireless networks are called by other names. You may hear the terms *peer-to-peer* or *ad hoc* networks to refer to these types of networks.

Peer-to-Peer Network - see also computer-to-computer and ad hoc.

Is a host PC the same as a network server?

No, a network server's main purpose is to manage network resources, such as users, passwords, applications, Internet connections and filtering, and so forth. It is not intended to be used as a personal computer to do everyday work on, such as word processing, spreadsheet analysis, and the like.

Configure Host PCs *(continued)*

Your host PC needs either a modem or an Ethernet adapter for Internet access and a wireless adapter card. If you share a dial-up Internet access with other computers in a computer-to-computer network, note that the connection speed becomes slower because each computer uses part of the available bandwidth.

For this reason, you may want to invest in a high-speed connection to the Internet, such as broadband, when you decide to set up a shared Internet connection.

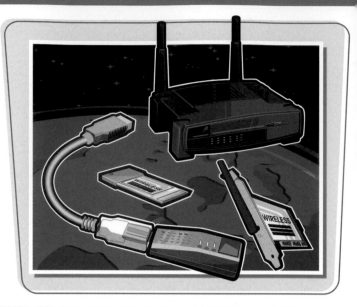

Configure Host PCs *(continued)*

The Advanced dialog box appears.

⑪ Click the **Computer-to-computer (ad hoc) networks only** option (○ changes to ◉).

⑫ Deselect the **Automatically connect to non-preferred networks** option (☑ changes to ☐).

⑬ Click **Close**.

The Advanced window closes.

⑭ Click **Add**.

Advanced ⟨?⟩⟨X⟩

Networks to access

○ Any available network (access point preferred)

○ Access point (infrastructure) networks only

◉ Computer-to-computer (ad hoc) networks only

☐ Automatically connect to non-preferred networks

[Close]

Wireless Network Connection Prope... ⟨?⟩⟨X⟩

General | Wireless Networks | Advanced

☑ Use Windows to configure my wireless network settings

Available networks:

To connect to, disconnect from, or find out more information about wireless networks in range, click the button below.

[View Wireless Networks]

Preferred networks:
Automatically connect to available networks in the order listed below:

[Move up]
[Move down]

[Add...] [Remove] [Properties]

Learn about setting up wireless network configuration.

[Advanced]

[Close] [Cancel]

The Wireless network properties dialog box appears.

⑮ Type a name for your network.

⑯ Click here and select **Disabled**.

⑰ Click **OK**.

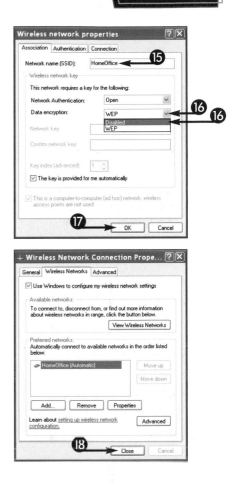

The Wireless network properties dialog box closes and Windows creates your network.

⑱ Click **Close**.

TIPS

When should I turn off data encryption?

If you turn off data encryption when you create your network, this makes it easier to configure your network. You should secure your wireless network once you configure it and confirm the client computers are communicating with your host computer. For more information on wireless network security, see Chapter 8.

Will I lose my Internet connection if the host PC is shut off?

Yes, you will. If this occurs frequently, consider accessing the Internet using a different host PC, if one is available to you. Or, discuss the situation with the owner of the host PC and he or she may schedule shut downs around the times you are not accessing the Internet.

Configure Client PCs

You must configure the client computers on your wireless network. Your client PCs connect to the Internet through the host computer.

Even without Internet access, your computers can share files and folders, printers, and other resources over a computer-to-computer wireless network. A wireless network without Internet access is more secure because unauthorized users cannot access your network from the Internet.

Configure Client PCs

1 From the Wireless Networking Connection Properties dialog box, click the **Internet Protocol (TCP/IP)** option (☐ changes to ☑).

Note: To open the Wireless Network Connection Properties dialog box, see the section "Configure Host PC."

2 Click **Properties**.

The Internet Protocol (TCP/IP) Properties dialog box appears.

3 Click the **Obtain an IP address automatically** option (○ changes to ◉).

Note: If this client PC will share an Internet connection through your host computer, you can skip to Step **7**.

④ Click the **Use the following IP address** option (○ changes to ◉).

⑤ Type a unique IP address for each client PC.

Note: *You can start by typing **192.168.0.2**, increasing the last number for each client PC, for example, **192.168.0.3**, **192.168.0.4**, and so on.*

⑥ Press Tab.

● Windows automatically fills in the Subnet mask number.

⑦ Click **OK**.

The Internet Protocol (TCP/IP) Properties dialog box closes.

⑧ Click **OK**.

⑨ Repeat Steps **9** to **18** in the section "Configure Host PCs" to create a computer-to-computer network with the same name on each client PC.

Your client PC is configured for computer-to-computer networking.

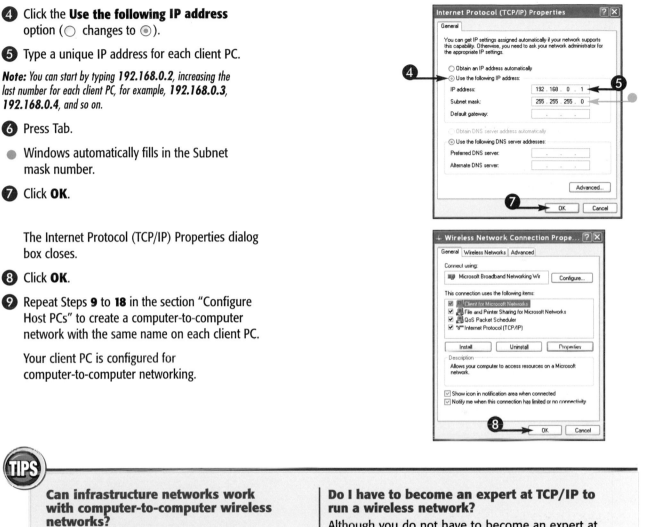

TIPS

Can infrastructure networks work with computer-to-computer wireless networks?

Yes, you can configure wireless network adapters for two modes, computer-to-computer and infrastructure mode. If the network adapter is configured to use infrastructure mode, then you can make it communicate with a computer-to-computer network.

Infrastructure Network

➕

Computer-to-Computer Network

Do I have to become an expert at TCP/IP to run a wireless network?

Although you do not have to become an expert at it — not many people are — you should become familiar with TCP/IP addressing schemes, such as public versus private addresses, default gateways, and subnet masks. Many resources, such as books and Web sites, are available and they can teach you TCP/IP basics. One Web site you can you look at is www.tech-pro.net/intro_tcp.html.

TCP/IP

Enable Internet Sharing

You can share an Internet connection with other users on your computer-to-computer wireless network. You must first enable Internet sharing on your host PC.

One concern with sharing Internet connections is security. You can install third-party firewall software that lets you control the information moving both in and out of your computer. The Windows XP firewall only protects against incoming Internet connections.

Enable Internet Sharing

① Double-click the **Network Connection** icon (🖳).

② From the Local Area Connection Status dialog box, click **Properties**.

Note: You should configure the wired network connection on your host PC, not its wireless network connection.

The Local Area Connections Properties dialog box appears.

③ Click the **Advanced** tab.

The Advanced tab appears.

④ Click the **Allow other network users to connect through this computer's Internet connection** option (☐ changes to ☑).

⑤ Click **OK**.

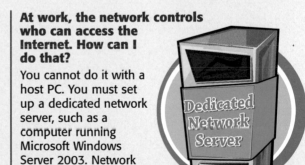

The Network Connections message box appears telling you that some settings may not take effect until the next time you connect to the Internet.

⑥ Click **OK**.

The Network Connections message box closes.

⑦ Click **OK**.

The Advanced Settings dialog box closes.

⑧ Click **OK**.

Windows enables Internet Connection Sharing.

 TIPS

How can I restrict who accesses the Internet when I am the host PC?

You cannot restrict computers that access the Internet through your host computer. Any client PC that is authorized to access your host computer over your computer-to-computer network shares the Internet connection.

At work, the network controls who can access the Internet. How can I do that?

You cannot do it with a host PC. You must set up a dedicated network server, such as a computer running Microsoft Windows Server 2003. Network servers allow you to grant privileges to users or groups of users, one of which can be Internet access.

CHAPTER 6

Software for Wireless Computing

A wireless computer is not worth much unless you can do something with it, such as create text documents, transfer files, surf the Web, and do other tasks. In this chapter, you learn about the many types of software you can use with wireless computers.

Discover Office Suites

You can share information between the programs in an *office suite* without performing manual conversions. An office suite is a collection of individual programs that enhance one another's functionality grouped into a bundle.

Many of today's office suites allow you to share and gather information while connected to a wireless network. For example, you can use the Microsoft Office Outlook e-mail program to communicate with others over a wireless network and Internet connection.

Parts of an Office Suite

The applications that come with an office suite depend on the software manufacturer. The most common set of applications in suites includes the following: a word processor, a spreadsheet program, a presentation program, an e-mail program, and a database program. Some other types of applications you may find include a graphics program for editing pictures, drawing programs, and Web page editors.

Word Processor

You use a word processor to create, edit, and view documents. The types of documents you can create with word processors include letters, envelopes, pamphlets, e-mail messages, Web pages, faxes, and more. Wireless network users can share word processing documents by saving them to a shared folder. To keep track of modifications, most word processors include revision marks that track additions, deletions, and comments. Wireless network users can keep a history of the types of changes they make to documents by keeping these revision marks enabled as they share documents.

Spreadsheet Program

Spreadsheet programs have an interface organized in rows and columns to group and organize information, much like a ledger book. You usually display accounting-type information, such as finances, product information, budgets, and costs. However, you can set up spreadsheets to display text, such as a contact management document with names, addresses, contact information, and notes. Most spreadsheets have a revision tool that tracks changes you make to the spreadsheet so you can share them with other network users. For example, you can create a spreadsheet for users to submit travel reimbursements with rows for inputting each travel item, such as meals, mileage, airfare, and so on. Users can save the file and send it to the accounting department for reimbursement.

Database Program

You use database programs to collect and organize data in a central location. You can then use reporting tools and other features to view and print your data. A database program lets you create relationships between data, reducing the number of times you must input a certain type of data. For example, when entering data about a family, you can use the same address and phone number for all family members. With the database, just type each family member's name and associate that name with the family's address.

Presentation Program

You use presentation software to give slide shows, usually with an overhead projector or from a Web page. With presentation software, you can create presentations for use during speeches, and for training classes, sales meetings, and marketing campaigns. Along with the standard slide that displays on a screen in front of the audience, you also have the option of printing handouts, posters, speaker notes, and other hard copies of your presentation.

E-Mail Programs

Office suites include e-mail programs to allow users to communicate with each other in a network environment. With a wireless network, you can attach to a server that has an Internet connection and send, receive, and manage e-mail messages. For more on e-mail programs, see the section "Understanding E-Mail Applications" as well as Chapter 7.

Understanding
E-Mail Applications

Electronic mail, or e-mail, applications let users communicate with each other using text-based messages. Users type messages and then send those messages to one or more recipients. Recipients can view the message, respond to it, store it in a folder for future reference, or delete it.

Most e-mail applications also include features that let you manage schedules, set up and track meetings, and create to-do lists.

E-Mail Messages

An e-mail message includes a few different parts: The *Address line* includes the e-mail address of the person you are sending the message to. The *From line* includes your e-mail address. The *Subject line* has an area to type a brief description of the message's content. The *Body* includes the full message.

Send Messages

After you create a message, you send it. The e-mail application reads the addresses in the address line and sends a copy of the message to each person listed there. Depending on the speed of your computer, network connection, and size of the message, the recipients can receive the message within a matter of seconds. This means you can sit at your computer in one country and send a message that someone across the globe can receive within five or ten seconds.

Store Mail

Once a message arrives, you can read it, delete it, or keep it. This is called storing mail. Typically, e-mail programs have *inboxes* in which new mail arrives. You can store messages in your inbox, but you may find sifting through a lot of messages tiresome and unproductive. Creating subfolders with descriptive names, such as the names of your projects, the departments with which you work, and storing your messages in them can help you organize.

Schedules

Many e-mail programs include calendar features that enable you to keep track of your daily, monthly, and yearly schedules. Some e-mail programs, such as Microsoft Outlook, enable you to set up and manage meetings from one place. You can create a meeting, send out invitations to participants, schedule a room or other resource, such as a projector, and set times for the meeting.

Tasks

You can use the task-scheduling feature in many e-mail programs to keep track of what you need to do. You can use this feature to eliminate papers lying around your desk, pinned to a bulletin board, or stuffed in your pocket.

Discover the Benefits of Web Browsers

When you connect to a wireless network that has Internet connectivity, you need software that lets you download and view content from the Web. This type of software is a *Web browser*.

View Web Pages

The main job of a Web browser is to allow you to view and navigate Web pages. Web pages can include text, pictures, animations, tables, charts, and other features. When you want to view a Web page, you type the Web browser's address in the address box. The Web page's address follows specific standards known as the Hypertext Transfer Protocol (HTTP).

Access Online Files

Another feature of Web browsers is file uploading and downloading. You can use a Web browser to connect to a file transport protocol (or FTP) site to send and receive files. An FTP site is set up like folders (or directories) you see in your My Computer folder, but the site is on a remote computer someplace on the Internet. You can connect to an FTP site in a Web browser, open My Computer, and then drag and drop files from the FTP site to your computer, or vice versa.

Navigate Hyperlinks

Another way to get to a page or a new site on the Web is to click *hyperlinks*. *Hyperlinks* are embedded navigation features that allow you to move from one page to another by clicking words or other linked items on a page. Text that is hyperlinked is usually underlined and starts as a blue color to help you find the link. When you click a link, an instruction is sent to the Web browser, directing it to download the page or picture that the hyperlink specifies.

View Pictures

With your Web browser, you can view colorful and entertaining pages that include pictures. Besides the ease with which users can navigate from page to page, the primary reason users love the Web is the availability of images you can view. Almost every site you visit on the Web includes a picture of some sort.

Access Multimedia Content

Another fascinating feature of the Web that most browsers support is multimedia. Multimedia content can include pictures, sound, video, or animation. One category of Web page that commonly includes multimedia is news-related Web sites. On these sites, you can find news articles, photos that supplement the news articles, and oftentimes video. You either view the video directly inside your Web browser or you download it and view it in a separate video program.

Transfer Files Using FTP

Many wireless networking users transfer files from one place on a network to another using *file transfer protocol*, or FTP. Although you can send and receive files using e-mail, using FTP to transfer files offers a few advantages.

For example, you can usually send files via FTP faster than through e-mail. Also, with FTP, you can dictate folders in which files are stored, allowing multiple users to access the files. With e-mail, you can send files only to a user's e-mail address, which is not publicly accessible.

Transfer Files Using FTP

① Click **start**.

② Click **All Programs**.

③ Click **Internet Explorer**.

The Internet Explorer window appears.

④ Type the address of an FTP site in the Address box.

⑤ Press `Enter`.

The Log On As window appears.

⑥ Type your username and password.

⑦ Click Log On.

Internet Explorer connects to the FTP site.

8 Double-click a folder on the FTP site.

The folder opens.

9 Click **start**.

10 Click **My Documents**.

The My Documents folder appears.

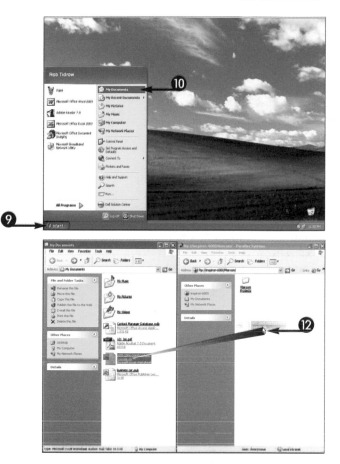

11 Position the FTP folder window and the My Documents window so both can be seen.

12 Drag a file or files from one window to the other.

The file transfers from the original folder to the destination folder.

TIPS

How do I know what my login username and password are?

Username and passwords for FTP sites are different than the ones you use to log in to Windows. The FTP site's administrator manages the username and passwords. You must request a username and a password from them. Some FTP sites, however, allow anonymous logins. This means anyone can access the FTP site's files and folders. Usually to gain access to anonymous FTP sites, simply enter *anonymous* in the username and your e-mail address for the password.

Does someone back up my folders on a wireless network folder?

It depends on who is running the site. In many cases, if the site that stores files is free, you should assume that the firm is not backing up your files. You may want to ensure you have copies of these files on a local computer of yours or on another type of storage media.

Synchronize Files

When you travel with your mobile computer, there are times when you cannot access the Internet, because you are not near a wireless access point, such as when you travel by car or bus, or when you visit a city that does not have public access.

However, you may need access to some Web pages even if you are not connected to the Internet. With the Synchronize tool, you can download Web pages to your computer while connected to the Internet and then review those pages while offline.

Synchronize Files

① Click **start**.

② Click **All Programs**.

③ Click **Accessories**.

④ Click **Synchronize**.

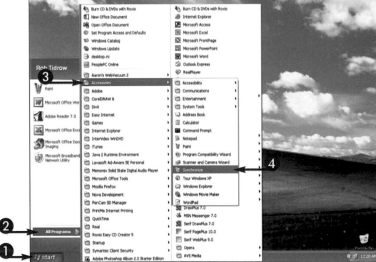

The Items to Synchronize window appears.

● This shows that the Web site is configured to download for offline access.

Your list may look different depending on the sites you have configured for offline access.

⑤ Click **Synchronize**.

The Synchronizing window displays the progress as the offline files are downloaded to your computer.

● The Progress tab shows the offline pages to download.

● Click Details to hide or show the Progress and Results tabs.

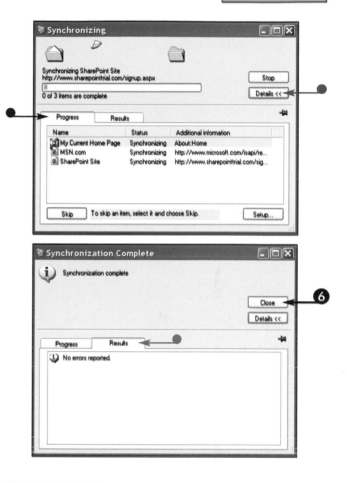

When finished, the Synchronization Complete window appears.

● The Results tab shows errors if your computer cannot access a Web page and download it for offline viewing.

⑥ Click Close.

Do I have to enable the offline access feature on my computer?

Yes, before you can start downloading pages for offline access, you must turn on offline file access. First, display **My Computer**. Then click **Tools**, click **Folder Options**, and then click the **Offline Files** tab. Click the **Enable Offline Files** option (☐ changes to ☑). Click **OK** to finish.

How long does it take to synchronize my offline files?

The time it takes to synchronize your offline files depends on how many Web sites you want to synchronize, the number of pages contained within those sites, and the speed of your Internet connection.

CHAPTER 7

Communicating with Wireless Computers

With a wireless computer, you can stay connected to your colleagues, supervisors, friends, and family while traveling. The most common way to communicate is using the e-mail program installed on your computer. However, as discussed in later chapters, Web-based e-mail programs are also available. Instant messaging is also a common business tool to allow you to do real-time chatting with coworkers, friends, and family.

Understanding the Types of Communication Software

Although e-mail is the oldest Internet and networking application, it is still the most popular tool on the Internet. Aside from e-mail, there are other tools you can use to communicate while you are using your wireless computer.

With e-mail you can create a message, send it to a list of recipients, and wait for a reply. One advantage of e-mail over the other types of communication software is that you can easily archive all the messages you send and receive.

E-mail Software

By default, most e-mail programs save the messages you receive from other users, as well as all the messages you send to others. E-mail programs can be stand-alone programs, such as Microsoft Outlook, or built-into other programs, such as Netscape Communicator's Netscape Mail utility. Netscape Mail utility is part of the overall browser program and does not work separately from it.

Web Mail

If you travel a great deal, consider opening an account with a Web mail provider. Web mail providers allow you to send and receive e-mail using a standard Web browser, such as Microsoft Internet Explorer or Opera. The reason Web mail is handy is that you can access your e-mail any time you have access to the Web. Just connect to the Web, type in the address to the Web mail provider, and start reading your mail. There is no need to set up a separate e-mail application to get your mail. In addition, you do not have to go through a complicated set of windows to set up servers, security options, and the like.

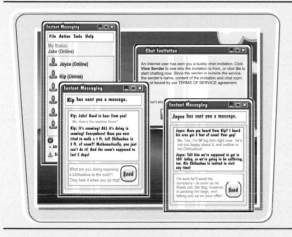

Instant Messaging Software

Because you communicate over the Internet in real-time, Instant Messaging (IM) software is like having a phone conversation with one or several participants. You can open up conversations with one or several other people. Sometimes you may have six or seven IM windows open on your desktop and be in different conversations with each one. Also, you can invite more than one person to be part of a conversation! IM software is available as part of Windows XP. You can purchase it separately, or download it from some Web sites, such as Yahoo! Messenger.

Video Messaging Software

A type of software that has been available for over ten years that is now just gaining solid ground is video messaging software. Video messaging software allows users to send and receive real-time messages using video as the medium. Most video messaging software uses other IM characteristics as well. For example, you can connect with another user (or multiple users) and communicate using video cameras and text. To use this type of software, you must have a video camera that supports video messaging and have a broadband or faster Internet connection.

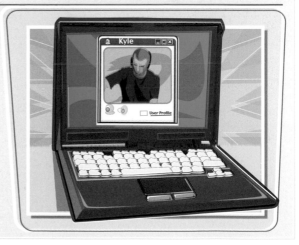

Configure Outlook Express E-Mail Software

Before you can begin composing, receiving, and sending e-mail messages, you must configure your e-mail software. During the configuration process, you set up user information, e-mail server information, and basic options.

Make sure you have an e-mail account set up with an Internet Service Provider (ISP) and that you have the following information handy during the configuration process: Your user name and password, your e-mail server name for receiving messages, and your e-mail server name for sending messages.

Configure Outlook Express E-Mail Software

① Click **start**.

② Click **E-mail Outlook Express**.

Note: This section assumes that you are using Outlook Express. If you are using a different software program, the steps are similar.

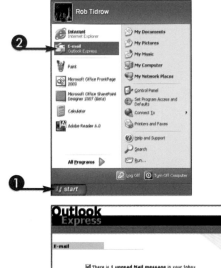

The Outlook Express window appears.

Note: If this is the first time you have set up an account, the Your Name Window appears. Go to Step 8.

③ Click **Tools**.

④ Click **Accounts**.

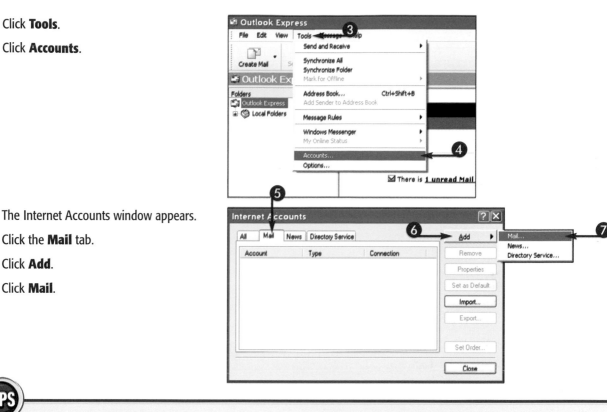

The Internet Accounts window appears.

⑤ Click the **Mail** tab.

⑥ Click **Add**.

⑦ Click **Mail**.

TIPS

Can I use a different e-mail program instead of Outlook Express?

Yes, a number of e-mail programs are available for you to use. Outlook Express is shown here because it is provided as part of Windows XP. Another program you may want to use is Microsoft Outlook, which is a program available in the Microsoft Office suite of programs. Although they are named similarly, Outlook Express and Outlook are not the same product.

Can I convert messages I received in Outlook Express to Microsoft Outlook?

Yes, when you are configuring Microsoft Outlook for the first time, the configuration program asks you if you want to move your Outlook Express messages to Outlook. Simply click **Yes** when asked.

continued

One disadvantage of using a standalone e-mail program like Outlook Express when you are traveling is that you may need to reconfigure it when you are accessing the Internet behind a firewall.

In addition, sometimes the firewall by which you are protected, such as when you access from a company Internet connection, does not allow you to access personal e-mail servers. In these cases, you must connect to the Internet from a different location to get your e-mail.

Configure Outlook Express E-Mail Software *(continued)*

The Your Name window appears.

⑧ Type your name.

⑨ Click **Next**.

The Internet E-mail address window appears.

⑩ Type your email address.

⑪ Click **Next**.

The E-mail Server Names window appears.

⑫ Click here and select POP3 from the My incoming mail server is list.

⑬ Type the name of your incoming server.

⑭ Type the name of your outgoing mail server.

⑮ Click **Next**.

The Internet Mail Logon window appears.

⑯ Type your username.

⑰ Type password.

⑱ Click **Next**.

TIPS

My incoming mail and outgoing mail server names are the same. Is this correct?

Yes, this is OK. Usually the names are different because different computers on the ISP side handle incoming and outgoing mail for security and filtering purposes. However, if the names provided by your ISP are the same, use those names. If, after you configure the e-mail account, you have problems connecting, contact your ISP and tell them you are having problems and inquire if you have the correct server names.

Can I have more than one e-mail account set up?

Yes. Click the **Mail** tab of the Internet Accounts window, click **Add**, and then click **Mail** to set up additional accounts just like you did in Steps **5** to **7** on the previous page. After you configure the new account, the name appears on the Mail tab with the first one you created.

continued

Each time you set up an e-mail account, you must go through this configuration process. This is true if you want to access email from a different computer. One thing you may want to do is to keep a copy of your e-mail configuration settings — username, incoming server name, and outgoing server name — in your wallet or address book. This way you can always access this information even when you are on the road.

Configure Outlook Express E-Mail Software (continued)

The Congratulations window appears.

⑲ Click **Finish**.

The Internet Accounts window appears.

● The new account appears on the Mail tab.

⑳ Click **Close**.

The Outlook Express window appears.

㉑ Click the plus sign (⊞) next to Local Folders.

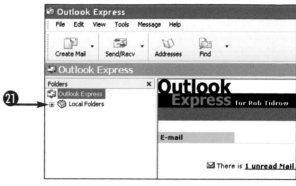

The e-mail folders for this account appear.

㉒ Click **Inbox**.

● The Inbox folder appears with its contents showing in the upper pane on the right side of the Outlook Express window and a sample message from Microsoft appears.

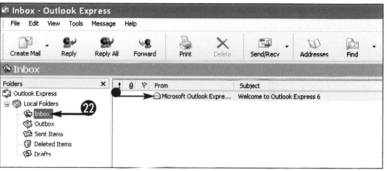

TIPS

Can I create a new folder in which to store my e-mail?

Yes, to do this, right-click a folder and click **New Folder**. In the Create Folder window, type the new folder name and click the folder under which you want the folder to appear. This makes the new folder a subfolder of the one you click. Click **OK**.

Can I store e-mail addresses in Outlook Express?

Yes, to do this click **Contacts** in the Contacts area in the lower left pane of the Outlook Express window. Click **New Contact**. In the Properties window, fill out the information on the **Name** tab. You do not have to fill out the other tabs, but you may want to in case you want to store detailed information about the contacts you enter. Click **OK**.

Using Outlook Express E-Mail Software

After you configure your e-mail software, you can download new messages from the e-mail server. Before you do this, however, you must connect to the Internet. Using the Send/Receive button, you can connect to your e-mail provider, send any messages you have in your Outbox, query the server for any mail stored there (new messages sent to you), and download the messages to your Outlook Express Inbox.

For more on configuring your e-mail software, see the section "Configure Outlook Express E-mail Software."

Using Outlook Express E-Mail Software

① Click the **Send/Receive** icon ().

● The Outlook Express window appears showing you the progress of downloading e-mail to your Inbox.

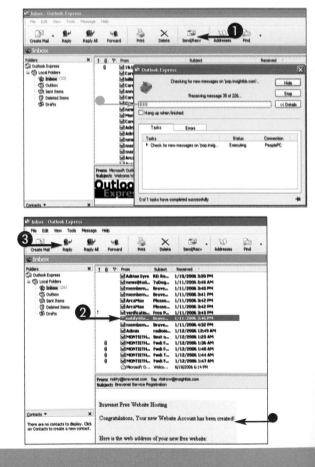

New messages appear in the Inbox folder.

② Click a message in the Inbox.

● The message text appears in the lower right pane of the Outlook Express window.

③ Click the **Reply** icon ( ).

The reply window appears for the message you are viewing.

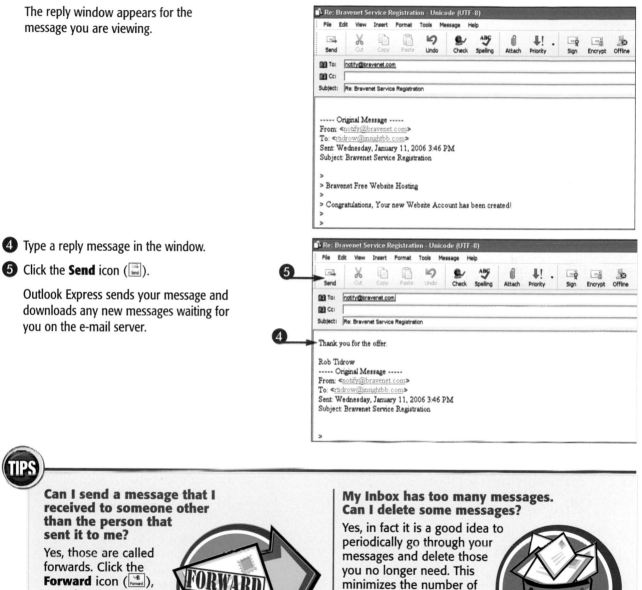

④ Type a reply message in the window.

⑤ Click the **Send** icon (📧).

Outlook Express sends your message and downloads any new messages waiting for you on the e-mail server.

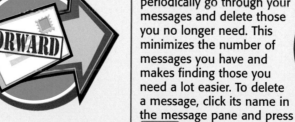

TIPS

Can I send a message that I received to someone other than the person that sent it to me?

Yes, those are called forwards. Click the **Forward** icon (📧), type the e-mail of the recipient who is to receive the message, and click 📧.

My Inbox has too many messages. Can I delete some messages?

Yes, in fact it is a good idea to periodically go through your messages and delete those you no longer need. This minimizes the number of messages you have and makes finding those you need a lot easier. To delete a message, click its name in the message pane and press **Delete**. This moves the message from the Inbox to the Deleted Items folder.

Set Up Web Mail

Many users use Web mail as their primary e-mail because it offers a few advantages over regular e-mail. It is easier to configure because you do not have to configure server names. Also, Web mail provides an interface that all Web users know how to use — the Web browser. This means you do not have to learn how to use a new program to read, send, and manage your e-mail.

Finally, Web mail is available from any place that you can access the Web. For example, if you travel and use a public computer, you do not have to set up and configure a separate e-mail program to access your mail. Simply use the Web browser. See the section "Using Outlook Express E-mail Software" for more information on regular e-mail. Although this example uses the Yahoo! Mail site, you can use these steps for other Web Mail providers.

Set Up Web Mail

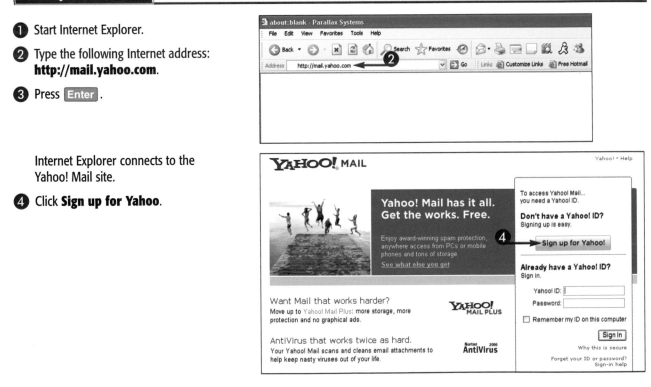

① Start Internet Explorer.

② Type the following Internet address: **http://mail.yahoo.com**.

③ Press Enter.

Internet Explorer connects to the Yahoo! Mail site.

④ Click **Sign up for Yahoo**.

The Yahoo! Registration page appears.

5 Fill out the registration information.

● The fields that have * (asterisks) next to them are required fields.

6 Type the code that Yahoo shows to verify your registration.

7 Click **I Agree**.

Your new account is set up.

Can I use the Web to download e-mail from my regular e-mail account?

Sometimes ISPs offer access to their e-mail accounts from the Web. If your ISP offers this feature, you need to find out the address of the Web mail server to which to connect to access your mail.

Are there other Web mail providers that I can use besides Yahoo!?

Yes, there are several available, some of which are free like Yahoo! Go to Yahoo! or Google and type in **web mail providers** in the search area to find other Web mail providers.

Using Web Mail

After you set up a Web mail account, you can start creating, sending, and receiving messages from there. Messages that you receive using your Web mail account are saved on the Web mail provider's server. That means if you receive a message using one computer and do not delete it from your Web mail account, you can see that same message using a different computer.

If you are using a regular e-mail program and server, you cannot do this because your messages are downloaded from the server to the computer from which you accessed the e-mail message. Although the following steps show how to use the Yahoo! Web mail service to read a new message, you can use these steps for other Web mail providers.

Using Web Mail

① After you set up a Web mail account (see Set Up Web Mail section), click **Continue to Yahoo! Mail**.

Note: For more on account set up, see the section "Set Up Web Mail."

The Yahoo! Mail page appears.

② Click the Inbox link.

The Mail tab appears, showing your Inbox and other message folders.

3 Click a message.

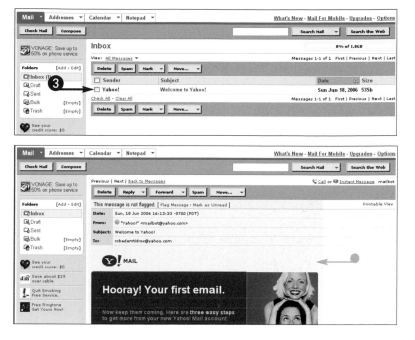

● The new message appears on the Mail tab.

How can some of these Web mail providers give me free e-mail?
The main way is through third-party advertisers. Advertisers pay to have ads placed on the pages where you view your e-mail messages.
In addition to advertisement sells, many Web mail providers offer premium features that you can subscribe to that cost a monthly fee. Usually the fee covers additional space for storing messages, extra features — such as a scheduling program for example — and ad-free messages.

How do I access the Yahoo! mail account if I am just starting out for the day?
To get to the Yahoo! mail page, type **mail.yahoo.com** in the Address bar of Internet Explorer. Once you connect to that site, you must type your username and password for your Yahoo! mail account. To have your computer store your name and username for future reference, click the **Remember Me** option (☐ changes to ☑).

Using Wireless Computers for Business Presentations

If you are a production manager, sales representative, or marketing director, it is not uncommon for you to be on the road a great deal of time. These road trips are often to help persuade potential clients or existing clients to purchase products or services. This chapter shows you how you can use your mobile computer to create, preview, and give Microsoft PowerPoint presentations to clients and potential clients.

Discover the Benefits of Powerful Presentations on the Go

A key to any business user on the go is to travel with and use software that mimics or duplicates the software on your office computer. One of the most popular programs to use during business travel is presentation software, such as Microsoft PowerPoint.

To help present sales ideas, products, advertising campaigns, and services, you often use multimedia presentations or demonstrations. If your job requires you to give presentations while out of the office, you need to master the slide show.

Presentation Software

The primary purpose of presentation software is to display information in easy-to-read pages. Presentation software includes tools to help you quickly and easily design colorful and interesting pages that allow you to present ideas, products, services, and other features of your company.

Slides

Presentation pages are called *slides*. Slides can include text, pictures, movies, Web pages, and more. In general, slides present information in a structure consisting of a title, body of the slide — where your information goes — and a footer. The footer often is information that gets repeated across all the slides, such as copyright information, date, and business name.

Views

Presentation software includes different views, which are displays of how you can see and work with your slides. For example, you can work on slides in the Normal view. With the Slide Sorter view, you can see small thumbnail views of your slides, making it easy to organize the order in which your slides display. Finally, the Slide Show view displays your finished slides.

Presentation Output

Presentation software allows you to output your slides on different media. The most prevalent way is to display the slides on a large screen using an LCD projector. Other output includes Web pages, color handouts, 35mm slides, speaker notes, audience notes, and color overheads. For some presentations, you may use a mixture of output — show the slides on a projector, print speaker notes for you, and print notes for the audience. You do this using the same presentation.

Self-Running Presentations

Presentations also can be delivered as self-running presentations, also known as kiosks. Kiosks can be set up to run automatically at sales booths, during intermission of a speech, and any place in which you want viewers to walk up and view the presentation without requiring someone to start and stop it. When running slide shows in kiosk mode, the presentation is shown at full screen.

Create a Slide Show

You can create presentations using two methods: You can create the presentation from scratch, or you can create the slide show using the AutoContent Wizard. Whichever way you use, you can choose a predefined template provided by Microsoft PowerPoint that provides the overall design of your presentation.

Templates help you establish the tone or feel of your presentation. For example, a business-oriented template could include professional-looking images, fonts, and colors. More entertaining templates, on the other hand, use playful images, fun fonts, and wild color schemes.

Create a Slide Show

1 Click **start**.

2 Click **All Programs**.

3 Click **Microsoft PowerPoint**.

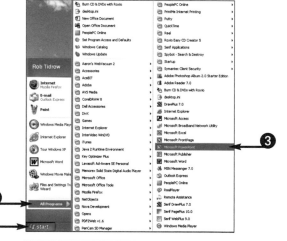

The PowerPoint window appears.

4 Click **From Design Template**.

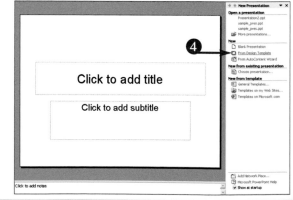

The design templates appear.

⑤ Click a design.

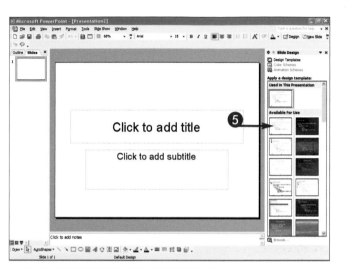

This example shows the Capsule design template.

⑥ To add a title to your new presentation, click inside the section called **Click to add title**.

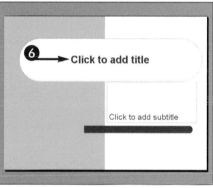

TIPS

How do I know what each template looks like?

You can look at the small thumbnail image of the design templates in the Slide Design pane. Although small, these tiny views give you a general idea of the colors, layout, and look of the design. You can also click a design and view it full size. If you do not like the design, click File and then Close to close the design.

Can I edit a presentation on the road?

Yes. In fact, you may find that you do this more often then not. For example, if you find a problem with a graphic while reviewing a presentation at the hotel the night before you visit a client, you can use your wireless capabilities to connect to the hotel's wireless network, access the Internet, and download a new graphic. Then you can insert the new graphic into your presentation.

continued

Before creating your slides, take a few moments to write down and organize your thoughts. When you add information to a slide, keep the text to a minimum. For example, you do not want so much information on a screen that you overwhelm the audience.

If a topic is too large for one slide — usually five or six bullet points — consider dividing the topic into two slides, spreading the remainder of the material onto a second slide. Try to balance each slide then. For example, if the topic has nine key points, put five on the first slide and four on the second slide.

Create a Slide Show *(continued)*

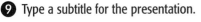

7 Type a title for the presentation.

8 To add a subtitle, click inside the section called **Click to add subtitle**.

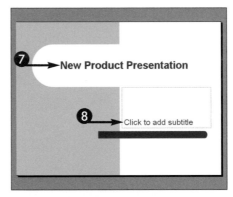

9 Type a subtitle for the presentation.

10 Click **New Slide**.

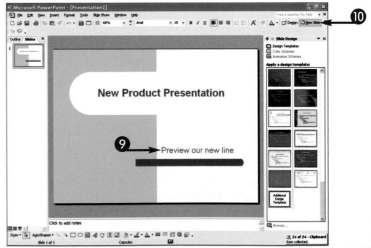

PowerPoint inserts a new slide in your presentation.

⑪ To add a title to the slide, click **Click to add title** and type a title.

⑫ To add text to the slide, click **Click to add text** and type text.

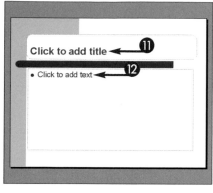

● Your text appears on the slide

● You can continue to add slides to the slide show by clicking **New Slide**.

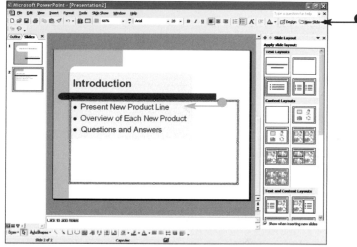

TIPS

When I finish creating a slide show, can I save it as a Web page?

Yes, to save the slide show as a Web page, click **File** and then **Save As Web Page**. In the File name box, type a name for the Web page. Click **Save**. The presentation is saved with a .htm format, which is one of the standard formats for viewing pages in a Web browser.

How many slides can I add to the slide show?

You can have as many slides in a presentation as you want. In most cases, you will want to limit the slide show to the number of slides you can present during a meeting or presentation.

Preview a Slide Show

You can preview your slide show to make sure it has no mistakes, testing and retesting the presentation so you know it works best. However, you generally want to do this while you are still in the office. To view your slide show on your laptop, use the Slide Show view. This plays your slide show just as if you are displaying it through a projector.

The reason that you want to preview a slide show while still in the office is because, there, you have access to supporting documents, images — for example, the company logo — as well as other resources that are not available to you while traveling.

Preview a Slide Show

① Open the slide show in PowerPoint.

② Click **View**.

③ Click **Slide Show**.

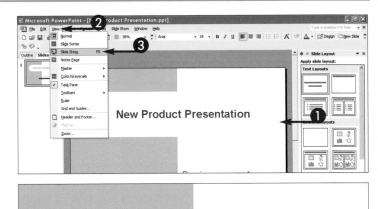

The presentation appears in the Slide Show view, which displays the slide the full width and height of the computer screen.

④ Click the mouse once to advance to the next slide.

The second slide appears.

5 Continue clicking to the end of the slide show.

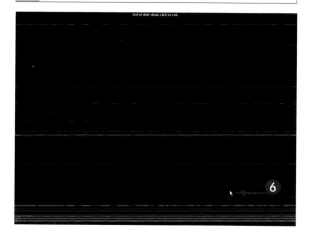

A black screen with instructions appears.

6 Click the mouse once.

The PowerPoint editing window appears.

TIPS

Can I pause the slide show before the end?

Yes. Many times while you are presenting a slide show to an audience, you may be asked to switch to another program, such as Internet Explorer. To switch to a different program that you have running in the background, press Alt+Tab to toggle to a different program.

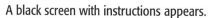

Can I return to a previously viewed slide?

Yes. You can move backward in a slide show by pressing Backspace, or right-clicking the slide and selecting Previous. If the mouse has a scrolling wheel, roll the scrolling wheel backward to move to the previous slide.

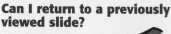

Discover Presentation Mechanics

Whether you are on the road doing a presentation in front of a new client or back in the home office showing slides to your team, there are a few presentation mechanics that can help you. These are some tips you can follow that help you make the most out of your presentation.

Timing

Know how long you are scheduled to present your slide show, and keep your presentation within that time frame. Practice your presentation using the slide show several times prior to the actual program. This is good to do the night before the meeting. Select **Slide Show** and then **Timings** to start a timer that tracks the length of time each slide stays on-screen as you practice. The timer also displays the entire time you spend on the presentation during practice.

Know Your Presentation

A boring way to present a slide show is to read each bullet point verbatim. Avoid this approach because your audience can read the items on the slide show. Instead, point out an item and then expand on it using your own knowledge. Think of it as reading between the lines.

Prepare for the Glitches

At times you will be asked to perform the impossible during a presentation, such as exiting the slide show and pulling up a Web site. Because you know this may happen, visit the meeting room prior to the meeting, check your wireless networking connection and test how well you can access the Internet. You can avoid other glitches by making sure your laptop's battery is fully charged — plug it into an AC outlet when you can — and making a backup of your presentation to a disc or other storage media in case you have to use another computer for the presentation.

Use a Pointer

One way to make your presentation appear more professional is to invest in a laser pointer. During your presentation, use the device to point out specific bulleted items, pictures, and other key highlights. With the pointer, you are free to move around the room as you discuss each slide.

Create Handouts

As you give your speech, you want the audience to pay attention to you. Take the time to prepare packets of handouts so audience members can jot down quick notes to your presentation, and don't have to transcribe everything you say. PowerPoint provides you with options for printing handouts with 1, 2, 3, 4, 6, or 9 slides to a page.

Using Wireless Computers for Entertainment

You can listen to music, play games, have conversations with other users, download news reports, or watch videos on your mobile computer while traveling. The Internet, the premier place to acquire the latest entertainment, has online stores that offer songs you can download to your computer or other digital device. These stores also have entire CDs of songs you can purchase without leaving your home or office. This chapter shows you how to use your mobile computer to stay entertained during those long trips away from home.

Register for Online Music

You can enjoy listening to music as you work by downloading music to your computer and playing it back using software such as Windows Media Player. You can obtain music from the Internet from a number of sites.

Although each site has its own downloading methods, you can follow the general steps in this section. If you are not sure how a site works, visit the site's FAQ — frequently asked questions — page or similar page to find downloading instructions.

Register for Online Music

① Start Internet Explorer.

② Type the address of the music store to visit, such as **music.yahoo.com**.

③ Press **Enter**.

Internet Explorer connects to the Yahoo! Music site and the Yahoo! Music Unlimited page appears.

④ Click the **Sign Up** link.

The Yahoo! ID page appears.

Note: *If you already have a Yahoo! ID, use it to sign on to the Yahoo! Music site and skip to Step* **9**.

5 Fill out the registration information.

● The fields that have * (asterisks) next to them are required fields.

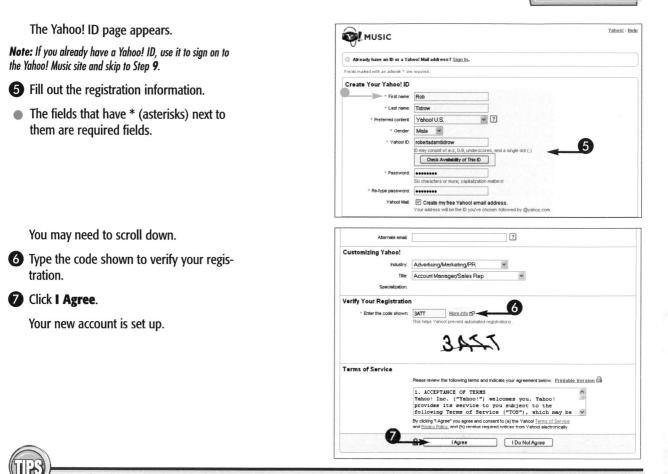

You may need to scroll down.

6 Type the code shown to verify your registration.

7 Click **I Agree**.

Your new account is set up.

---

continued

TIPS

Do regular stores offer music over the Internet?

Yes. In fact, Wal-Mart runs one of the larger Internet music stores. At musicdownloads .walmart.com, you can purchase music to download, listen to free samples of music, and sign up to receive updates of your favorite artists. Other retail stores that offer music downloads include Sam Goodies and Tracks.

I thought I could download music for free. Why do I have to pay for music?

There are some file-sharing programs available that enable you to share files with other users. In turn, you can obtain files from users who use this same type of software. The files that are shared are sometimes illegally swapped, including music and video files. You should protect yourself from potential prosecution by visiting music download sites that are reputable and require you to pay for each song.

When you decide to join a music download site, you may want to look for sites that offer more than just the music.

For example, some sites, such as the Yahoo! Music site, provide updates on the latest music, with categories ranging from hip-hop to classical; news about your favorite artists; music videos; free samples of recently released music; and photographs of groups and artists.

The Registration Completed page appears.

8 Click **Continue to Yahoo! Music**.

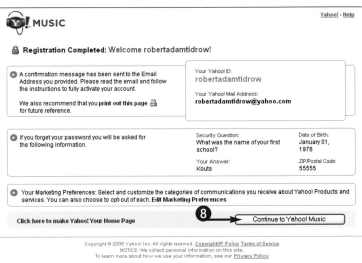

The Welcome to Yahoo! Music page appears.

9 Click **CONTINUE**.

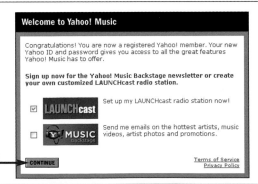

The Yahoo! Music page appears.

● You can click here to download the free music player software.

● You can search for the latest music, ranging from hip-hop to classical, using these fields.

● You can click these links to download photographs of groups and artists.

● You can click here to download free samples of recently released music.

● You can click here to view news about your favorite artists.

● You can click these links to view music videos.

TIPS

Can I download ring tones for my cell phone from these music sites?

Yes. Often, online music sites also offer ring tones for your phone. Just like some online music offers, sometimes you can find free or reduced-cost ring tones for a trial period to enable you to try out the ring-tone feature of the site before you invest in a long-term subscription.

Can I watch music videos from all online music sites?

No. Some online music sites are simply that — warehouses for digital music. Many times the sites that do offer music videos have some kind of business relationship set up with the music video companies to have rights to carry those videos. If you are interested in music videos with your music, visit Yahoo! or Google and search for sites that offer music downloads and music videos.

Download the Yahoo! Music Engine

Many times a music site offers music files in proprietary formats. This limits the opportunities for users to download music and then sell or share those music files with other users. To play these music files usually requires the user to download a separate player, which most sites offer free.

The following steps show how to acquire the Yahoo! Music Engine available from the Yahoo! Music site. This program enables you to create playlists, rip and burn CDs and DVDs, share playlists with other users, and download music from the Yahoo! Music site.

Download the Yahoo! Music Engine

1 Type the address **music.yahoo.com**.

The Yahoo! Music home page appears.

Note: To register on this site, see the section "Register for Online Music."

2 Press `Enter`.

3 Click the **Downloads** tab.

4 Click **Free Player**.

The Yahoo! Music Engine page appears.

5 Click **Install Free**.

The Install the Yahoo! Music Engine page appears.

6 Click **Get Started**.

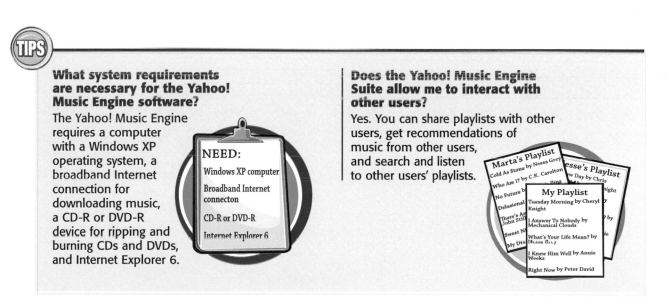

The File Download window appears.

7 Click **Save**.

TIPS

What system requirements are necessary for the Yahoo! Music Engine software?

The Yahoo! Music Engine requires a computer with a Windows XP operating system, a broadband Internet connection for downloading music, a CD-R or DVD-R device for ripping and burning CDs and DVDs, and Internet Explorer 6.

NEED:
Windows XP computer
Broadband Internet connecton
CD-R or DVD-R
Internet Explorer 6

Does the Yahoo! Music Engine Suite allow me to interact with other users?

Yes. You can share playlists with other users, get recommendations of music from other users, and search and listen to other users' playlists.

continued

You must download the ymesetup.exe file to start the process of acquiring the Yahoo! Music Engine Suite. You can then execute the file so you can select options for the suite.

You can download just the music engine or download additional programs that can enhance your online experience. One program you can download with the Yahoo! Music Engine Suite is Yahoo! Messenger instant messaging service, for example.

The Save As window appears.

⑧ Click **Save**.

The ymesetup.exe files is downloaded to your computer's desktop.

⑨ Click the Minimize icon (■) on Internet Explorer.

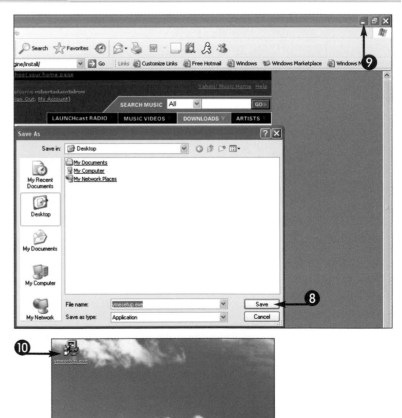

The desktop appears.

⑩ Double-click the **ymesetup.exe** file.

The Yahoo! Music Engine Suite Installation window appears.

⑪ Answer the questions on the six-page wizard to download and install the Yahoo! Music Engine Suite, clicking **Next** to advance through the pages.

In the pages of the wizard, you are prompted to make Yahoo! your default search and home page.

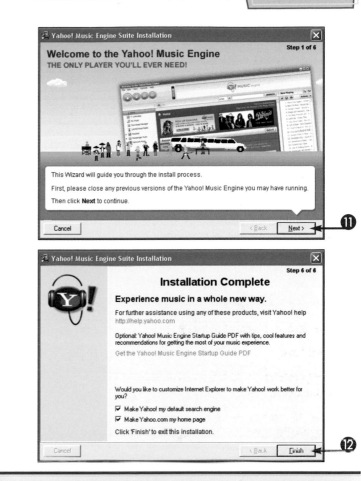

When finished, the Yahoo! Engine Music Suite Installation window appears.

⑫ Click Finish.

Note: *If you are prompted to shut down and restart Windows, click Yes to do so.*

TIPS

What is the Open File — Security Warning window that appears?

This is a window that displays on some systems if you turn on security settings on your computer. If you do not see it, the security setting has been disabled or lowered on your computer. The security warning tells you that software is being installed on your computer. You can cancel the action if the software is something you deem to be offensive or may possibly cause problems on your computer.

Can I remove the Yahoo! Music Engine Suite from my computer when I no longer need it?

Yes. Use the Add/Remove Programs tool in the Control Panel. Click **Start**, and then **Control Panel**. Click **Add/Remove Programs**, and click the **Yahoo! Music Engine** listing. Click **Remove**.

Using Yahoo! Music Unlimited

Once you set your system up with the Yahoo! Music Engine Suite, you can start enjoying music and other features of the Yahoo! Music Unlimited site. For new subscribers, there is a seven-day free trial period and then you must pay a monthly or annual charge for access to the songs. You also pay a small fee for each song that you download.

When you travel with your computer and have the Yahoo! Music Engine Suite installed, you can simply start it up and begin downloading and listening to your favorite music.

Using Yahoo! Music Unlimited

① Click the **Start Yahoo! Music Engine** icon () on the taskbar.

The Welcome to the Yahoo! Music Engine window appears.

② Click **Next**.

The Add Your Music window appears.

③ Click the **No, do not add my music at this time** option (○ changes to ◉).

④ Click **Next**.

The Setup Complete. Get Started Now window appears.

5 Click **Finish**.

The Yahoo! Music Engine window appears.

6 Type the name of a music artist in the search box.

7 Click **Search**.

● A list of music available for download by that artist appears in the window.

8 Drag music items from the middle pane to the right pane.

Yahoo! Music Engine creates a playlist of songs.

9 Click the **Play** icon (◉) to download and play back a song.

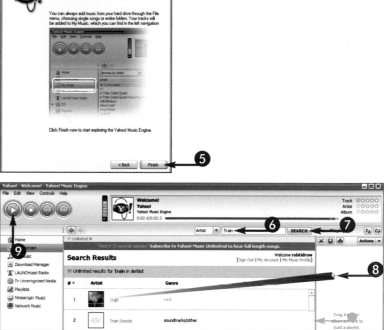

TIPS

Do I have to give my credit card information to Yahoo! for a free sample?

Yes. Like most online services that offer a free trial, Yahoo! does require a credit card number up front. This enables Yahoo! to set up an account in your name as soon as your trial period is over. Of course, you are allowed to cancel the subscription before the trial ends so that your credit card is not billed a monthly subscription fee.

Can I download my music to an MP3 player?

Yes. That requires additional fees that you must pay to Yahoo! Music. To see what these charges are, visit music.yahoo.com/unlimited/.

Discover Weblogs (Blogs)

Another form of entertainment that many mobile users enjoy is Weblogs, or blogs. *Blogs* are sites that enable users to post messages to a Web page that others can read and respond to.

Electronic Journals

Weblogs are similar in nature to the long-running newsgroup feature that has been available on the Internet for many years. The main difference is that blog messages end up on Web pages specifically designed for this type of communication. Threads of conversations are saved for readers to view later if they are not actively participating. Also, entries are saved in reverse chronological order so you can read the latest entries first.

Web Diaries

For many users, blogs are a way to keep track of their daily lives and offer that information to anyone who is willing to read it. These are usually known as Web diaries, replacing the traditional paper-based diaries of the past. Some diary blogs are open to comments from readers.

Blogospheres and Public Discourse

Blogs have become a way for many public discussions to happen. For example, politicians have created *blogospheres* — sites at which blogs take place — for concerned citizens to voice their opinions about current events.

Popular Political Blogs

As you travel with your mobile computer, blogs are an excellent way to stay in touch with others around the world. Some of the more popular political blogs are AndrewSullivan.com, Ron Gunzburger's Politics1.com, and Taegan Goddard's Political Wire.

Company Blogging

Some companies have started using blogs to promote communication among their employees. Blogs can streamline communications for a project team and allow workers to express suggestions for improvement, and provide a way for all employees to get to know each other. However, some companies have released employees who maintain personal blogs where they discuss company matters.

Discover Streaming Radio

Another entertainment media you might enjoy while you travel is streaming radio. *Streaming radio* enables you to listen to radio stations over the Internet. Many commercial and public radio stations offer their programming as streaming media.

Streaming Radio Software

To listen to streaming radio, you must have streaming radio software installed. Internet radio software enables you to locate and listen to Internet radio stations. When you use Internet radio software, they usually search for available stations and list them in categories, such as: '70s Soul & R&B, Americana, Classic Rock, Country, and Hip-Hop.

Find Radio Software

You can find good radio software at the following sites:

Software name	Web site
iRadio	www.3alab.com/download/iRadioSetup.exe
CleanSofts	www.cleansofts.com/find/streaming_radio.html
AudioStreamer Pro	www.rmbsoft.com/programs/aspro21.exe
Internet Radio Ripper 2.0	www.zheadware.com/download/irripper.exe

Buffer Files

Streaming radio uses buffering technology to push out chunks of data over the Internet. This enables all users, even those not set up with broadband Internet, to access the data without being overwhelmed by file sizes. Depending on connection speed, overall Internet traffic, and local bottlenecks — such as how many programs a user is running — users may experience some gaps or delays in programming as a user's computer is receiving the data from the Internet.

Find Stations

Not all radio stations offer streaming radio programs. You usually have to look for them. However, once you find them, you can access them anytime you are on the Internet, regardless of their proximity to you. One way to find stations is to use an online radio station location, such as the Radio-Locator at www.radio-locator.com. Here you can find stations by ZIP code, call letters, or country.

Public Broadcasts

A number of public broadcast stations offer their programs as streaming audio. Usually the audio file is available after the live program has aired, enabling users to access the streaming files if they miss the regular program. For example, the following public stations offer streaming audio of their shows: Indiana Public Radio, Muncie, Indiana; KERA, Dallas, Texas; KIPO/Hawaii Public Radio, Honolulu, Hawaii; KMUW, Wichita, Kansas; Minnesota Public Radio News; WAMU, Washington, D.C.

Discover Online Gaming

Business travel can be a mixed bag of sorts. You may enjoy it because it enables you to get away from the office and interact with different people, but it can be lonely and boring at times. If you travel with your mobile computer and have Internet access, such as through a wireless network, you may enjoy spending time playing online games.

Online Gaming Sites

A number of sites are available that enable users to play their favorite games online. Visit the Ogaming site at www.ogaming.com to find links to hundreds of online games. You can play some games, such as Online Solitaire, by yourself, while others are more fun and challenging when you play them against someone, such as Internet Chess.

Play Network Games

Some online games are designed to be played in a multiplayer format in which multiple players from different locales meet via the Internet to play a single game. Some of these games can take days or even months to finish.

Available Games

As you travel with your mobile computer, you may want to know what types of games are available for you to join. Some of these games include *City of Heroes*, *Dungeons & Dragons*, *Everquest 2*, *Guild Wars*, and *Vanguard*.

Play Poker

Perhaps playing chess or *Dungeons & Dragons* is not your idea of a great evening. However, playing several hands of Texas hold 'em is! One of the hottest trends recently has been online poker. Hundreds of poker sites have appeared online, such as PokerRoom.com, Pacificpoker.com, and Paradisepoker.com. These sites allow users to play poker against other users from all over the world. Visit PokerListings.com at www.pokerlistings.com for the latest list of online poker site.

Online Tournaments

Many poker sites offer online tournaments for users to win prizes. Some poker sites include online tournaments to allow you to qualify for live tournaments in Las Vegas, Hawaii, Atlantic City, and other locations. These tournaments are called *satellite tournaments*. The World Series of Poker has seen players who gained entry through online tournaments actually win the real-life event. To get more information about these tournaments, visit PokerStars.com at www.pokerstars.com.

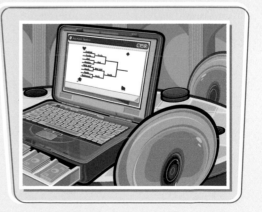

Working on Wireless Networks

The main reason for creating, connecting to, and administering a wireless network connection is to use it to get your work done. You can use wireless networks to share files, store and retrieve files in remote folders, and access devices in remote locations. In larger networks, you can even set up electronic mail servers to help users communicate with one another. This chapter teaches you how to browse your network, share a folder with other users on your network, and select a network printer.

Understanding Wireless Network Services and Resources

Most network users want to work with a number of common network services like printers, applications, and sharing and accessing files. This section describes common network services.

Printers

Sharing relatively expensive equipment such as printers is one of the primary reasons that networks are useful. Using wireless networks makes it easier to share network printers because it is not necessary to attach a printer and computer using a common cable system.

Share Files

You can easily use a wireless network to share the files on your computer with other users on the network. You can also allow other users to work on files stored on your computer.

Access Files

You can store files that you access on a network on another user's computer or on a computer that is dedicated to storing files for all the users on the network. This type of computer is called a *file server*. Accessing file servers on a network often involves the use of authentication schemes such as user names and passwords. Storing files on a server provides benefits, including enabling multiple users to modify a single document, allowing centralized backup support, and providing a central warehouse for your important files.

Application Servers and Databases

You can store some applications on a computer network from which you can access and run the program. These computers, called *application servers*, usually control larger, more complex tasks, such as running a database program, managing the data in the database, or managing a document warehouse.

Multimedia Servers and Document Warehouses

Two important types of application servers are a multimedia server and document warehouse. A multimedia server lets you store and view digital movies from one location. With document warehouses, a single program can store all the documents for a company and allow those documents to be edited and viewed from that storage environment.

Connect to a Wireless Network

You can connect to your wireless network by using a few different methods. One way is to boot up Windows XP so that it automatically searches for and connects to a preferred network.

Another way is to connect to the network using a shortcut in the Windows XP start menu. This is called *forcing a connection*. You may need to connect or reconnect to a wireless network after you install new hardware or when your connection is disabled or interrupted.

Connect to a Wireless Network

① Click **start**.

② Click **Connect To**.

③ Click **Wireless Network Connection**.

The Wireless Network Connection Status dialog box appears.

④ Click **Close**.

⑤ Position the mouse cursor over the **Network Connection** icon () in the system tray.

● A text box appears, indicating the computer is connected to the wireless network.

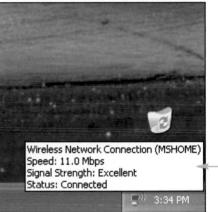

How do I view all my network connections?

You can view all of your network connections by clicking **start**, **Connect To**, and then **Show all connections**. A Network Connections window appears, showing all your network connections.

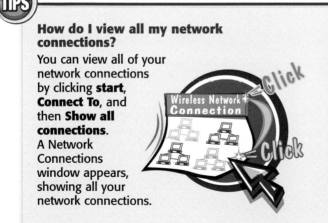

My system does not have the Connect To link as described previously. Why not?

If you do not have administrator privileges on your computer, you may not see this link. The administrator for your computer may have it disabled for all non-administrators.

Browse a Network

You can use My Network Places to view the computers connected to your wireless network. My Network Places can appear in several places within Windows XP. You can open My Network Places from an icon on your desktop, from an icon on the Start menu, and from a folder in My Computer (or Windows Explorer)

My Network Places displays drives, folders, and files available on the network. You can access files, folders, and other information that is available to you on the wireless network.

① Click **start**.

② Click **My Network Places**.

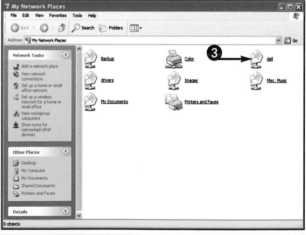

The My Network Places window appears.

③ Double-click a network folder (📁).

The shared network folder opens displaying its contents.

④ Double-click a subfolder (📁).

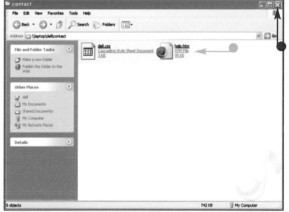

● The subfolder opens, displaying its content.

● You can click the **Close** icon (❌) to close the window.

TIPS

When I try to access a file, it is not available. What do I do?

If you attempt to access a file or folder and it is not available, the computer that stores the information may have been removed from the network or is simply turned off. Check to see if the computer that is sharing the file or folder is turned on and connected to your wireless network.

Why does it take so long to browse the network?

When you browse the network, Windows checks network connections for all protocols configured on your computer. If Windows does not find something right away, it keeps looking for a set period of time, such as 120 seconds or even longer. Check the protocols that you have configured and remove any that you do not need.

Share a Folder

You can share your files and folders with other users on your wireless network. This allows other users to access information on your computer that you choose to share.

When you share a folder on your wireless network, other users can view all the files within that folder. For this reason, share only those folders you want others to access. You should not share personal, confidential, and sensitive files with other users. Put those kinds of files in nonshared folders.

Share a Folder

1 Click the folder (📁) you want to share on your wireless network.

2 Click the **Share this folder** link in the task pane of the window.

The Properties dialog box for your folder appears.

3 Click the **Sharing** tab.

4 Click the **Share this folder on the network** option (☐ changes to ☑).

5 Type a name for the folder.

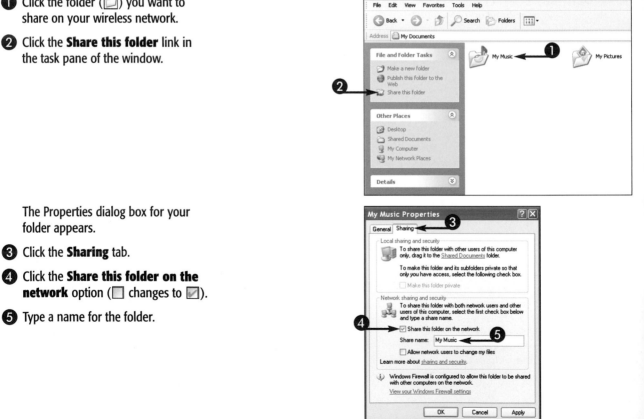

6 Click the **Allow network users to change my files** option (☐ changes to ☑) if you want to enable other users to modify files in this folder.

7 Click **Apply**.

8 Click **OK**.

● A hand () appears in the icon representing a shared folder.

The folder is now available to other network users.

To stop sharing a folder, perform Steps **1** to **8**, skip Step **5**, and uncheck the options in Steps **4** and **6**.

How do I hide a folder from other users?
You can hide a folder by adding a dollar sign ($) to the end of the share name. For example, you can hide a folder named Photos by renaming it as Photos$. However, network users who know or can guess the folder name can still access the hidden folder. You can assign a drive letter to a hidden folder, making it easier to access on the network.

Can I log in to a hidden folder from another computer?
Yes if you know the exact name of it (including the $ part) and where it is located. Keep in mind, though, most organizations have a policy against accessing private files that are stored on company computers. If you work for a company that has such policies and you purposely violate that policy, you can be dismissed.

Monitor Shared Folders

You can monitor the folders that you share on your wireless network. Windows XP enables you to view which shared folders are being used, the path of the shared folders, and how many users are connected to a shared folder.

You must have administrator privileges to monitor shared folders.

Monitor Shared Folders

① Click **start**.

② Click **Control Panel**.

The Control Panel window appears.

③ Click the **Performance and Maintenance** icon (🖳).

The Performance and Maintenance window appears.

④ Click the **Administrative Tools** icon ().

The Administrative Tools window appears.

⑤ Click the **Computer Management** icon (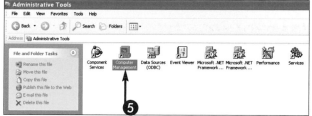).

I tried to access a folder, but cannot open it. Why is this?

There are some files and folders that you cannot share on your wireless network. You cannot share files in your Documents and Settings, Program Files, and Windows system folders. You also cannot share folders that belong to other users.

Can I share programs with other users?

Usually you cannot unless the program is specifically designed to work as a shared network program and you have the correct licensing to share the program with multiple users.

continued

As an administrator, you can see a list of shared folders and determine the number of users who are currently accessing the folders. Monitoring the number of users who are accessing the folders on your computer helps you to determine if it is appropriate for you to perform tasks, such as removing or changing shared files, or even turning your computer off.

When you need to shut down your computer or perform file maintenance, send e-mails to the users with access to your shared folders to warn them. Give the users a specific amount of time – for example, "in 10 minutes" or "at 1:00 P.M." – to allow them to disconnect from the shared folders.

Monitor Shared Folders *(continued)*

The Computer Management window appears.

6 Click the plus sign (⊞) beside the Shared Folders folder.

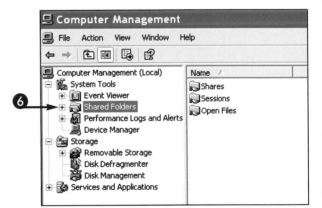

A list of subfolders appears.

7 Click **Shares**.

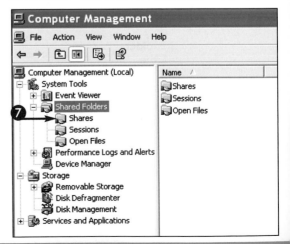

● A list of shared folders appears, listing folder names, folder paths, and the number of users connecting to the shared folders.

● When you finish reviewing the information, you can click ☒ to close the Computer Management window.

How do I unshare a folder?

To unshare a folder, navigate to the folder icon, right-click the folder icon, and select **Properties**. Then click the **Sharing** tab and select the **Share this folder on the network** option (☐ changes to ☑).

Can I lock out certain users from my files?

Yes, but you have to set up a password on the shared folder, and then give that password only to those users you want to access your files.

Assign a Letter to a Network Folder

You can assign a drive letter to a folder located on your wireless network. Assigning a letter to a folder makes it easier and faster to access a folder.

Drives letters begin with A and go to Z. Letters A–F are typically used by devices on your computer: A for a floppy drive, B for a second floppy drive, C for the hard drive, D and E for CD/DVD drives, and F for removable media.

Assign a Letter to a Network Folder

① Click **start**.

② Click **My Computer**.

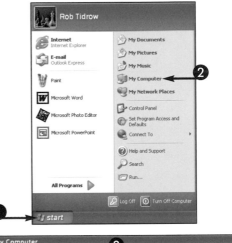

The My Computer window appears.

③ Click **Tools**.

④ Click **Map Network Drive**.

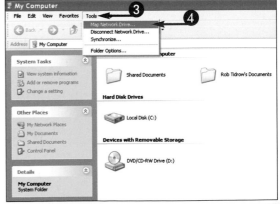

The Map Network Drive Wizard appears.

5 Click here to display a list of the available drive letters.

Map Network Drive

Windows can help you connect to a shared network folder and assign a drive letter to the connection so that you can access the folder using My Computer.

Specify the drive letter for the connection and the folder that you want to connect to:

Drive: Z:

Folder: | Browse...

Example: \\server\share

☑ Reconnect at logon

Connect using a different user name.

Sign up for online storage or connect to a network server.

< Back | Finish | Cancel

A list of available drive letters appears.

6 Click the drive letter you want to assign to a folder.

7 Click **Browse** to locate the folder on your network to which you want to assign a drive letter.

Map Network Drive

Windows can help you connect to a shared network folder and assign a drive letter to the connection so that you can access the folder using My Computer.

Specify the drive letter for the connection and the folder that you want to connect to:

Drive: Z:

Z:
Y:
X:
W:
V:
U:
T:
S:
R:
Q:
P:
O:
N:
M:
L:
K:
J:
I:
H:
G:
F:
E:
B:
A:
(none)

Browse...

Cancel

TIPS

What drive letters should I use?

You should use a drive letter from M to Z. You should reserve letters A to J for your floppy disk drive, local hard drives, CD-ROM drives, DVD drives, and other storage devices.

I do not have a B drive. Why not?

B drives were used for second floppy disk drives until CD-ROMs and DVDs became popular drives. B drives were commonly 5 1/4 inch floppy disks.

continued

Although drives begin with A and go to Z, typically, network administrators like to start assigning drive letters in reverse order to leave enough contiguous letters for these local devices.

You can access a network folder the same way you access a folder located on your computer. You can easily access a folder shared by computers in your workgroup. A workgroup is a group of related computers on your network.

Assign a Letter to a Network Folder *(continued)*

The Browse For Folder dialog box appears.

Windows automatically highlights your current network workgroup.

8 Click the workgroup that contains the folder to which you want to assign a drive letter.

The computers in the workgroup you selected appear.

9 Click the name of the computer to which you want to assign a drive letter.

The folders on the computer you selected appear.

⑩ Click the name of the folder to which you want to assign a drive letter.

⑪ Click **OK**.

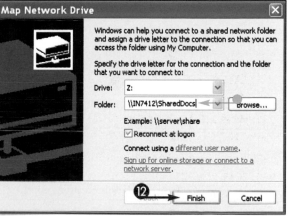

● The Map Network Drive wizard displays the folder you selected.

⑫ Click **Finish**.

Windows assigns the drive letter to the folder.

You can now access the folder the same way you access local drives, such as a hard drive.

 TIPS

Do I have to set up my drive letters each time I start Windows?

No, folders to which you assign a drive letter automatically connect every time you log on to your computer. However, you can configure Windows not to do this if you do not want your computer to automatically connect to the folders. Before performing Step **12** in this section, you can deselect the box beside Reconnect at logon (☐ changes to ☑) if you want to disable the feature.

One of my programs sometimes prompts with an error message that it cannot find a drive. Why is that?

Usually it means that a network drive was not re-established under Windows when you started your computer. The drive, for example, may have been unavailable at that time. Sometimes you can open My Network Places and enter the drive letter in the Address line to force a connection to that drive.

Add a Network Printer

You can use a printer that is attached to another computer on your wireless network. Sharing a printer with other users on your wireless network saves money and space.

To share a printer, the printer must be one that is manufactured to allow sharing. Although most printers are of this kind, do not assume all of them are. Contact the manufacturer or research the printer before purchasing it to make sure it is one you can share on a network.

① Click **start**.

② Click **Printers and Faxes**.

The Printers and Faxes window appears.

③ Click the **Add a printer** link.

The Add Printer Wizard screen appears.

4️⃣ Click **Next**.

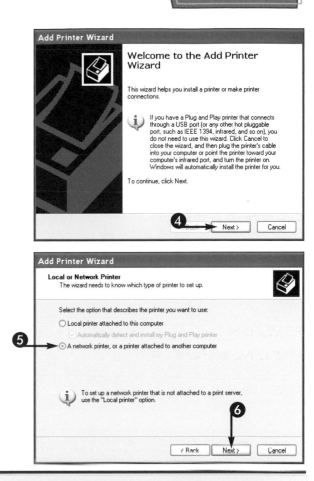

The Local or Network Printer screen appears.

5️⃣ Click the **A network printer, or a printer attached to another computer** option (○ changes to ⊙).

6️⃣ Click **Next**.

Can I set up a default printer that is on the network?

Yes, you can add and select additional printers, making them available for your use on a wireless network. The first printer you add becomes your default printer, which is automatically used unless you specifically select another printer. Your default printer displays a check mark in its icon.

What should I do when I am not connected to the network but I want to print the next time I connect?

Simply select the print command in the program from which you want to print — such as clicking **File** and then **Print** in Word — and send the print job to the printer. Windows stores the print job in the offline printer folder until the next time you re-connect to the network. You can then print.

continued

All the network printers that you add are available for your use. You can use most applications on your computer to print to a network printer. Before you print, take the time to know exactly where that printer is. That way you do not print documents to a printer that is located in a different building, across campus, or in a locked office.

Also, make sure the printer uses the type of paper on which you need to print. Some printers use plain paper, while others use specialized paper. If you are using a printer attached to another user's computer, you should get permission before using the printer.

Add a Network Printer (continued)

The Specify a Printer screen appears.

7 Click the **Browse for a printer** option (○ changes to ◉).

8 Click **Next**.

The Browse for Printer screen appears.

9 Click the printer you want to add.

10 Click **Next**.

A Windows message box appears, asking you to confirm that you want to add a printer.

⑪ Click **Yes**.

The Completing the Add Printer Wizard dialog box appears.

⑫ Click **Finish**.

Windows adds the printer you selected.

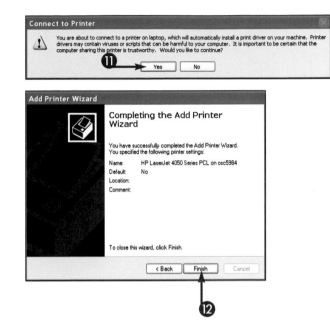

 TIPS

Is there anything I need to do to print to a network printer?

As long as a shared printer is functioning and correctly connected to the wireless network, you can use the printer. Some printers may require intervention, such as adding paper or ink, which prevents the printer from being used until it is serviced.

I sent a print job to a network printer, but want to cancel it. How can I do that?

If you are quick enough, click **start**, and then **Printers and Faxes**, and double-click the icon for the network printer. Select your print job and click **Document**, and then **Cancel**.

Administering Wireless Networks

Because maintenance is an important part of any network, you should perform it on a daily, weekly, monthly, and annual basis. Consider creating a journal or task log to track all the administration tasks you must do if you are in charge of a host PC on a wireless network. In this chapter, you learn how to add and delete users, change user passwords, and perform other administrative functions.

Establish User Accounts

Wireless networks typically require all users to have their own user account before they can access the network. User accounts provide the initial way for a network system to guard against unauthorized entry into the network resources. When you set up accounts on your network, consider how large the user base may become.

If a small group of people uses the system, first names or even nicknames may suffice, as long as others who are added later do not share names with existing members. A good system for networks that expect to grow is to use first initial and last name, first name_last name, or a similar naming convention.

Authentication

The primary purpose of user accounts is to allow the computer to verify that the person accessing the computer is the person who is authorized to do so. The most common way of accomplishing this is to require each user to have his or her own individual login ID, or username, accompanied by a password.

Restrictions

You can use user accounts to restrict the network services and resources that a user can access. These services and resources may be on the computer on which the user is logged on. Most networks place restrictions on the services and resources that users can access to better manage the network and increase security.

Special Accounts

There are a number of user accounts on a computer that may not represent an actual person. For example, a computer may have an account called *backup* that is used solely by a backup application. Two other common special accounts are the guest account, for temporary users of a computer, and the administrator account, which manages the computer.

Groups

On networks, user accounts are typically arranged into groups to make the management of users easier. For example, a group called *Internet* can contain the names of users who may access the Internet. Users not listed in this group cannot access the Internet using the network.

Administration

User accounts, whether on a computer or a network, require an administrator to create and manage those accounts. An administrator has a special designated user account that gives him or her the capability to manipulate user accounts. On a large network, you can have many administrators managing the network and the user accounts.

Add a User Account

You can add a user account to a computer to enable different people to access the computer and the wireless network. Windows XP associates settings for that new user on the computer. For example, each user can have a unique desktop, start menu, wallpaper, and Internet favorites folder. Each user also can have a different picture for his or her user account.

Each user that wants to log in to your network needs his or her own username and password. You can set up user accounts using the User Accounts program in Windows XP.

Add a User Account

① Click **start**.

② Click **Control Panel**.

The Control Panel window appears.

③ Click the **User Accounts** icon (■).

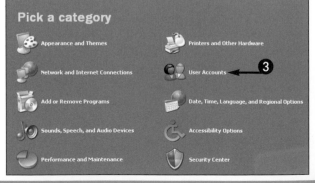

The User Accounts window appears.

④ Click **Create a new account**.

The Name the new account screen appears.

Windows does not let me create a new user account. Why not?

Not everyone can create a new user account in Windows XP. To create a user account, you must log in using a computer administrator account. You use computer administrator accounts to perform maintenance tasks on the computer, such as managing user accounts.

I forgot my password. How can I log on?

You cannot log on without an authorized password. If another user can access your computer, such as with an administrator username and password, ask him or her to log in and then change your password to one that you can use.

continued

Each user on a computer should have his or her own user account to help keep files and information, such as e-mail messages, organized. For shared computers like this, set up a different user name for each person. This way, when each user logs in, specific settings for that user, including network settings, and folders, are accessible to that user.

Many companies and schools reduce expenses by using shared computers. Instead of purchasing one computer for each person, an organization can purchase one computer for many people.

Add a User Account *(continued)*

⑤ Type a name for the new account.

⑥ Click **Next**.

Name the new account

Type a name for the new account:

Tamika

This name will appear on the Welcome screen and on the Start menu.

Next >   Cancel

The Pick an account type screen appears.

⑦ Click the type of account you want to create (○ changes to ●).

Note: *You should create a Limited account type for users who are not computer administrators.*

Pick an account type

◉ Computer administrator   ○ Limited

With a computer administrator account, you can:
- Create, change, and delete accounts
- Make system-wide changes
- Install programs and access all files

< Back   Create Account   Cancel

8 Click **Create Account**.

Pick an account type

○ Computer administrator ◉ Limited

With a limited account, you can:
• Change or remove your password
• Change your picture, theme, and other desktop settings
• View files you created
• View files in the Shared Documents folder

Users with limited accounts cannot always install programs. Depending on the program, a user might need administrator privileges to install it.

Also, programs designed prior to Windows XP or Windows 2000 might not work properly with limited accounts. For best results, choose programs bearing the Designed for Windows XP logo, or, to run older programs, choose the "computer administrator" account type.

[< Back] [Create Account] [Cancel]

The User Accounts window appears.

● An icon appears next to the username to indicate an account has been created.

8

User Accounts

Pick a task...

→ Change an account

→ Create a new account

→ Change the way users log on or off

or pick an account to change

Rob Tidrow
Computer administrator

Tamika
Limited account

Guest
Guest account is off

TIPS

How many accounts can I set up?

There is no limit to the amount of user accounts you can create. However, you should keep the number of accounts at a manageable level.

How do I change my account to an administrator account?

You can change from a limited to an administrator account from the User Accounts window. Click the account name and select the **Change an account** link. Then select Administrator and click Change my account type.

Delete a User Account

Windows XP enables you to create as many users as you want on a computer. However, you should keep the number to a manageable one; say, no more than a half dozen. You can remove a user when you get too many users or have a user who no longer uses this computer.

You can delete accounts for users who no longer need access to your computer or your wireless network to conserve computer resources and increase network security.

Delete a User Account

① Click **start**.

② Click **Control Panel**.

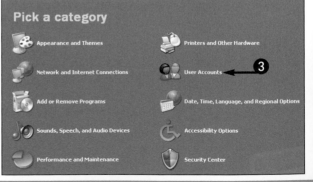

The Control Panel window appears.

③ Click 🖳.

The User Accounts window appears.

④ Click the account you want to delete.

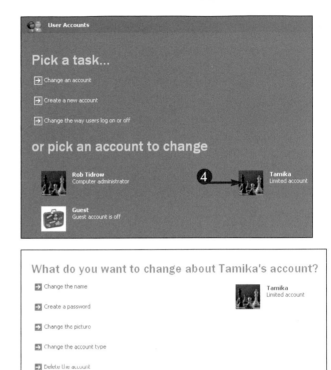

Windows asks what you want to change about the selected account.

continued

TIPS

What happens after I delete a user account?

When you delete a user account, Windows XP asks if you want to delete the files belonging to that user account. If you delete those files, the files belonging to the deleted user account are permanently deleted.

Can I undelete a user I have deleted?

No, once the user is removed, you cannot undelete it. To re-enable that user to access your network, simply create a new user.

A computer must always have at least one administrator account authorized to create and delete user accounts. If you work in an area in which a person is responsible for the maintenance and management of computers, have just one administrator for each computer.

However, if the computer is in a remote area where one administrator is not always around to fix problems on a computer, set up several administrators on each computer. This way, more than one person is responsible for the computer maintenance and management.

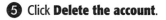
Delete a User Account *(continued)*

⑤ Click **Delete the account**.

What do you want to change about Tamika's account?

→ Change the name

→ Create a password

→ Change the picture

→ Change the account type

→ Delete the account

Tamika
Limited account

A screen appears asking if you want to keep or delete the user's personal files.

⑥ Click **Delete Files**.

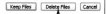

Do you want to keep Tamika's files?

Before you delete Tamika's account, Windows can automatically save the contents of Tamika's desktop and "My Documents" folder to a new folder called "Tamika" on your desktop. However, Windows cannot save Tamika's e-mail messages, Internet favorites, and other settings.

[Keep Files] [Delete Files] [Cancel]

Windows asks you to confirm that
you want to delete the account.

7 Click **Delete Account.**

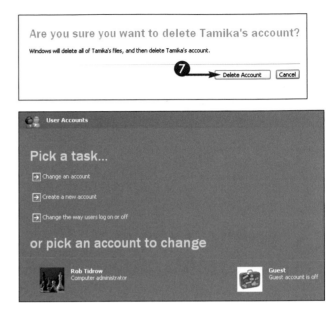

Are you sure you want to delete Tamika's account?

Windows will delete all of Tamika's files, and then delete Tamika's account.

7 → Delete Account   Cancel

The User Accounts window appears
displaying the list of remaining user
accounts.

The account you removed is gone.

User Accounts

Pick a task...

→ Change an account

→ Create a new account

→ Change the way users log on or off

or pick an account to change

Rob Tidrow
Computer administrator

Guest
Guest account is off

TIPS

What if I do not delete the files belonging to the account that I want to delete?

If you choose not
to delete the files
belonging to a user
account that you
are deleting, the
files belonging to
the deleted user
account are placed
into a folder on the
Windows desktop.

Can I open files from a deleted user?

Yes, locate the folder for
the deleted user on the
Windows desktop. The
files are stored there.

Assign a User Password

Assigning a password for each user account secures your wireless network by preventing unauthorized access to computers connected to the network. Avoid using easily guessed passwords, such as your name or username, or common words or names. Most secure passwords have seven or more characters, with a mix of lowercase and uppercase letters, numerals, and symbols.

Another habit you should get into is to change your password periodically. Some companies require their employees to change passwords every 30 days, for example.

Assign a User Password

① Click **start**.

② Click **Control Panel**.

The Control Panel window appears.

③ Click .

The User Accounts window appears.

④ Click **Change an account**.

The Pick an account to change screen appears.

⑤ Click the account for which you want to assign a password.

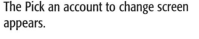

 TIPS

I tried to bypass the login screen to access my computer, but Windows does not let me. What should I do?

Windows XP does not allow you to access your computer without a password after a user account and password are set up. Unlike Windows versions in the past, such as Windows 98, you cannot click Cancel to bypass the login screen. You must log in with a valid username or password.

Can you give me some examples of good passwords?

Some of the best passwords are ones that combine two unrelated words or terms, using mixed uppercase and lowercase letters, and includes one or more numbers. Examples include rEd97next, heAR0Forty, and zer0camErA.

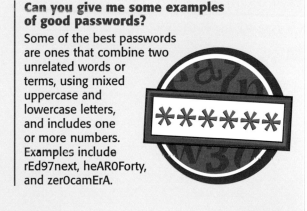

continued

Try to avoid writing your password down or letting other users know your password. If you must keep a list of your passwords, ensure they are in a safe location.

One thing you may do is write the password and place it in your wallet or purse. Then if you need a reminder of your password, look in these places for it. Do not write it down and place it under your keyboard, in your top desk drawer, or hang it on your monitor. These are the first places people look for it.

Assign a User Password *(continued)*

A screen appears asking what you want to change about a specific account.

6 Click **Create a password**.

The Create a password for your account screen appears.

7 Type a new password.

8 Type the password again to confirm.

9 Type a word or phrase that will help you remember the password.

10 Click **Create Password**.

What do you want to change about your account?

→ Change my name

6 → Create a password

Rob Tidrow
Computer administrator

→ Change my picture

→ Change my account type

→ Set up my account to use a .NET Passport

Create a password for your account

Type a new password: **7**
••••••••

Type the new password again to confirm: **8**
••••••••

If your password contains capital letters, be sure to type them the same way every time you log on.

Type a word or phrase to use as a password hint: **9**
The town where you were born

The password hint will be visible to everyone who uses this computer.

10 → Create Password   Cancel

A screen appears asking if you want to make your files and folders private.

⑪ Click **Yes, Make Private**.

This protects your files from other users of the computer.

A screen appears asking what you want to change about a specific account.

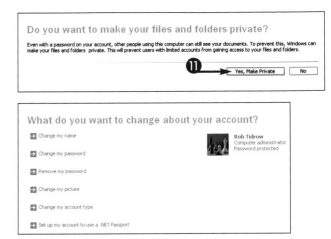

Do you want to make your files and folders private?

Even with a password on your account, other people using this computer can still see your documents. To prevent this, Windows can make your files and folders private. This will prevent users with limited accounts from gaining access to your files and folders.

⑪ → [Yes, Make Private]   [No]

What do you want to change about your account?

➔ Change my name
➔ Change my password
➔ Remove my password
➔ Change my picture
➔ Change my account type
➔ Set up my account to use a .NET Passport

Rob Tidrow
Computer administrator
Password protected

TIPS

What do I do if I forget my password?
If you cannot remember your password and therefore cannot log in to your account, a user with a computer administrator account will have to delete the password from your user account. After it is deleted, you can create a new password.

Should the administrator write down all passwords for their users?
No, the administrator should not do this. Written records of these passwords are considered confidential information by many organizations. If an unauthorized person accesses a document with written passwords, security breaches can ensue.

Activate a Guest Account

The Guest account is a permanent account that is added to your computer when you install Windows XP. You cannot remove it, but you can inactivate it. In fact, when you first install Windows, the Guest account is inactive.

You may find times when it is good to have it turned on. You can activate the Guest account on your Windows XP computer to enable temporary users to access your computer and network. Another reason to activate the Guest account is to use it to test your network's file and printer sharing settings after you get those items set up.

Activate a Guest Account

① Click **start**.

② Click **Control Panel**.

The Control Panel window appears.

③ Click 🖼.

The User Accounts window appears.

④ Click **Guest account**.

A screen appears asking if you want to turn on the Guest account.

5 Click **Turn On the Guest Account**.

● A screen appears indicating the Guest account is now active.

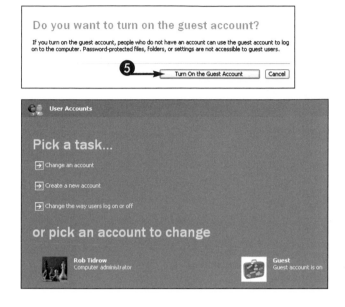

Do you want to turn on the guest account?

If you turn on the guest account, people who do not have an account can use the guest account to log on to the computer. Password-protected files, folders, or settings are not accessible to guest users.

5 ⟶ [Turn On the Guest Account] [Cancel]

User Accounts

Pick a task...

→ Change an account

→ Create a new account

→ Change the way users log on or off

or pick an account to change

Rob Tidrow
Computer administrator

Guest
Guest account is on

TIPS

Do I need to worry about security with a guest account?

Yes. Anytime a user, even a guest user, can access your computer, you can run a risk. Users who log on to your computer using the guest account cannot access password-protected files, folders, and settings, however, for security reasons, you may want to turn on the guest account only when necessary.

Can I change the picture for the guest account?

Yes. Open the User Accounts screen and select Guest. Select the Change the picture link and select a different picture. Select Change Picture.

You must have workgroups to enable users to connect to the resources available on it. Workgroups are analogous to departments — such as administration, sales, and marketing — in a large company. The workgroup name must be the same on all computers on a wireless network.

If necessary, you can change the workgroup name on a computer that you add to a wireless network so it can easily communicate with the other computers on the network. If you are connecting to a wireless network and are not sure of the workgroup name, ask someone what it is. Without the workgroup name, you cannot access shared resources on the network.

Change a Workgroup Name

① Click **start**.

② Click **Control Panel**.

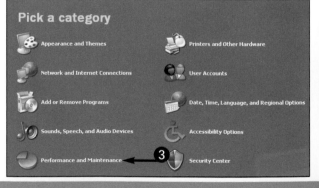

The Control Panel window appears.

③ Click the **Performance and Maintenance** icon ().

The Performance and Maintenance window appears.

④ Click the **System** icon ().

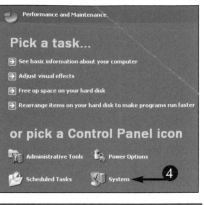

The System Properties dialog box appears.

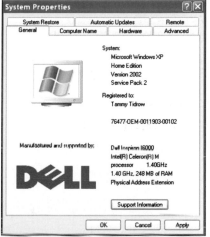

 TIPS

What should I choose as a workgroup name?

When choosing a workgroup name, try to keep workgroup names logical. For example, try using *sales* for the sales department or *home* for a home network. Make sure your workgroup names are short and do not contain spaces.

After I change the workgroup name on my computer, no one else can access my network. Why?

Make sure you inform the other users on your network about your workgroup change. Each user must change his or her workgroup name to match your workgroup name to ensure the network resources are available.

continued

Wireless networks can consist of computers using multiple workgroup names. You can change the workgroup name of your computer to access the resources of the different workgroups.

If you travel a great deal with a laptop and connect to wireless networks in various places, you need to become comfortable changing workgroup names. Each network may have different users attached to it and you will want to connect to those resources by knowing which resource uses what workgroup name and then change your settings to match that name.

Change a Workgroup Name *(continued)*

⑤ Click the **Computer Name** tab.

⑥ Click **Change**.

The Computer Name Changes dialog box appears.

⑦ Click in the Workgroup field and edit the workgroup name.

⑧ Click **OK**.

Windows accepts the new workgroup name.

A dialog box appears, welcoming you to your new workgroup.

9 Click **OK**.

A dialog box appears informing you that you must restart the computer.

10 Click **OK**.

The workgroup name is changed.

Note: *You must reboot your computer for the changes to take effect.*

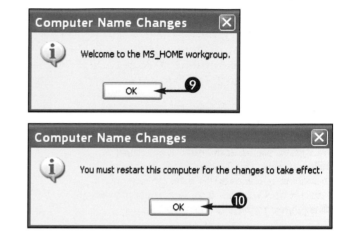

<hr />

TIPS

Does my workgroup network have a domain?

No. Larger computer networks use domains instead of workgroups to organize computers. If your computer requires you to join a domain, you must consult with the network administrator for instructions on how to access the domain.

Do I have to specify a workgroup?

Yes. You must belong to a workgroup to be on a network. If there are no other workgroups on the network you want to join, you can make up your own workgroup name, creating a workgroup with just one computer — yours.

Share Information on a Wireless Network

After you connect to a wireless network, you can share information in your folders on your computer with other users on the wireless network.

You must set up the folders you want to share by specifying each one. If you want to share several folders, but do not want to set up shares for each one individually, create one primary folder and then move the other folders into this primary one. This makes the moved folders subfolders. When you share the primary folder, all subfolders are shared as well.

Share Information on a Wireless Network

1 Click **start**.

2 Click **My Documents**.

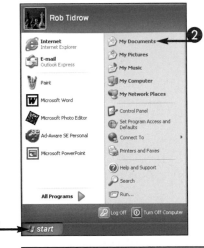

The My Documents window appears.

3 Click the folder (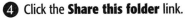) you want to share.

4 Click the **Share this folder** link.

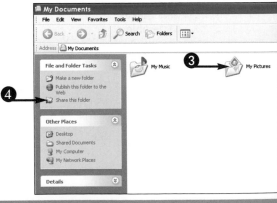

The Properties dialog box for the folder you selected appears.

5 Click the **Sharing** tab.

6 Click the **Share this folder on the network** option (☐ changes to ☑).

7 Type the name of the shared folder as it will appear on the network.

● You can click the **Allow network users to change my files** option (☐ changes to ☑) if you want to allow others to change the files.

8 Click **OK**.

● A hand (🤚) appears under the folder icon to indicate a shared folder on the wireless network.

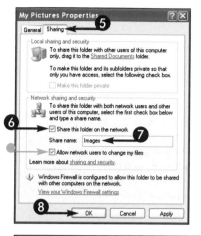

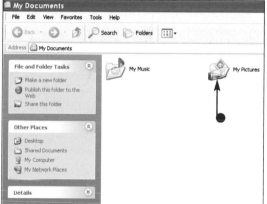

TIPS

Should I allow users to modify my shared files?

Allowing users to change your files lets them delete files as well. It also makes your files vulnerable should someone gain unauthorized access to your wireless network. Only allow users to change your files if the information is not essential or if you have current backups of the shared information.

Can I share music from my computer?

Yes. Store the music in a folder such as the My Music folder. You must store shared music in a separate folder from music you do not want to share. Set up a folder share for the music folder you want to share.

Share a Printer on a Wireless Network

One way to save money in your organization or home is to use one printer among several users. You can share your printer that is attached to your computer with other users on a wireless network.

When you share a printer on a wireless network, you attach the printer to one computer. You then set up the printer as a shared printer so others can connect to it over the network. The other computers must configure Windows to work with this shared printer. A shared printer shows up in your Printers and Faxes folder with a hand icon next to the printer icon.

Share a Printer on a Wireless Network

 Click **start**.

② Click **Printers and Faxes**.

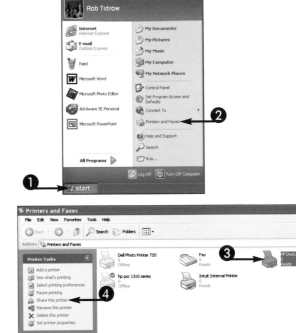

The Printers and Faxes window appears.

③ Click the printer you want to share.

④ Click the **Share this printer** link.

The Printer Properties dialog box appears.

5 Click the **Sharing** tab.

6 Click the **Share this printer** option
(○ changes to ⊙).

7 Type the name of the printer as you
want it to appear on the network.

8 Click **OK**.

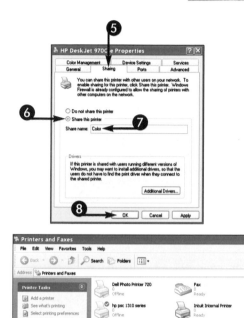

● A appears under the printer icon to
indicate a shared printer on the wireless
network.

TIPS

How do I access a wireless printer on the network?

Most operating systems have an easy way for users to locate and print to network printers — even those on a wireless network. To access a printer using a Windows XP computer, users can use the Add a Printer Wizard available from the Printers and Faxes window task pane.

Can I share my scanner like I can my printer?

In most cases, you cannot share scanners across a network. Some higher priced scanners do have network capabilities. Contact the scanner manufacturer to inquire about the make and model of your scanner and if it supports network scanning.

Securing Wireless Networks

Although one of the greatest concerns with wireless networks is how to keep data and resources secure, you can prevent security problems by doing a few simple things. In this chapter, such security features as WEP encryption, SSID names, firewalls and software, such as Windows help you stop unauthorized traffic originating from both the Internet and from within your own network.

Understanding Network Security

When you set up and use a network, including a wireless network, consider creating a security policy. This policy is to be enforced on all users who use your network. There are many components to a good security policy. All network administrators should evaluate each aspect of their network security.

Some of the policies you may consider include data encryption, unique hardware identification, Internet restrictions, and data filtering. Almost all medium to large companies are required (usually through shareholders or corporate officers) to document and adhere to strict security policies.

Encryption

A common way to protect information during its transmission, regardless of how the information is transmitted, is to encrypt it. *Encryption* takes the information and scrambles it so that it is unreadable. Only the intended recipient of the information has the code that allows the data to be unscrambled.

Identification

Each piece of equipment connected to a network is unique and is identifiable by its unique identification number required to connect to the network. It is possible to restrict network access to only those devices of which you are aware. This prevents any unauthorized equipment, such as another computer, from accessing your network without specific permission.

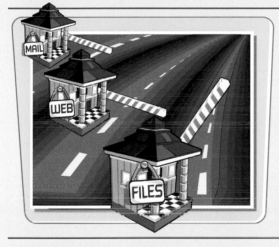

Filter Data

All data on a network is formatted into very specific types of data. For example, the information in an e-mail message is very different from the information you use to log on to the network. You can restrict the type of data on a network to prevent unauthorized users from using different data types to access the network. For example, if you never access the World Wide Web on your network, you can disable the transmission of Web pages over the network. Filtering programs also enables you to filter the type of content users can access over the Internet. For example, you can restrict access to the Web sites that meet certain criteria, such as violence, sexual themes, or drugs. Filtering software also lets you track user activity, including which user visits a specific site.

Restrict Sources

All information on a network contains the identification of the computer sending the data and the identification of the computer receiving the data. If needed, you can restrict the information that transfers on your network depending on the identification of the source. For example, you can restrict access to files located on the Internet. This prevents users on the Internet from attempting to access your network files. You can also restrict which computers transfer files to your network, reducing potential threats to your network's security.

Discover Benefits of Security

Implementing a sensible security policy on your wireless network has two major benefits: secure resources and protected data. When you create a security policy, be ready to present it to all your employees or users. In addition, have regular meetings to discuss, update, and amend security policies as your network grows and becomes more popular.

With an up-to-date security policy, companies can limit the amount of liability they may be responsible for, especially if they store sensitive client or customer data. You should also audit the security policy over time to ensure it is still effective.

Secure Resources

One of the primary reasons that people make attempts to access wireless networks is so that they can obtain access to the Internet. Without a proper security policy in place, unauthorized users can use your wireless network, thereby restricting the speed at which your network can transmit information.

Data Protection

Unauthorized access to your network leaves your data open to others. Apart from actually deleting or otherwise corrupting your data, the unauthorized user may copy your sensitive data and use it inappropriately, such as selling credit card numbers you stored on your computer to others.

There are two primary disadvantages to implementing a comprehensive security policy: management and usage speed. As with any type of rule or set of rules, security policies can get in the way of some users who want to access and use your network. In fact, some users may not use your network over time if the security policy is too rigid.

Do not be discouraged by this, especially if you do not want your network resources and data comprised.

Management

Planning, implementing, and maintaining a security policy is a very time-consuming process requiring the attention of the network administrator. Not only do you have to implement the security policy, but you must also stay abreast of the latest developments in wireless security to ensure your network does not become vulnerable.

Speed

One of the trade-offs of implementing a security policy is the speed at which the network operates and a user can work. If it is necessary to encrypt data, it takes longer for the data to travel between computers. Requiring users to use a password to access resources such as the computer files and printers reduces the speed at which users can work.

Understanding Threats to Network Data

One of the benefits, and at the same time a disadvantage, of wireless networks is that they broadcast information over a large geographic area, sometimes in excess of two or three miles. While this enables devices to communicate easily in many different locations, it also allows unauthorized persons to access that information.

Most persons trying to access your wireless network are looking for access to the Internet, but some may want to access your network's data. Because wireless networks work off of radio signals, anyone in your area with a receiving device (a laptop computer with a wireless card, for instance), can receive those signals.

Lax Security Procedures

Wireless networks all use some security in the form of passwords and identifications that allow only specific, authorized devices to connect to the wireless network. Unfortunately, many network administrators fail to take the time to properly implement a wireless network security process, making it that much easier for security breaches to happen.

Eavesdropping

By far the most common threat to a wireless network is in the form of eavesdropping on the signal, which the wireless network generates and which extends beyond the property of the network owner. For example, a wireless network in an office may transmit signals through the building wall to a location next door. The equipment an intruder can use to eavesdrop on wireless networks is the same that you use to construct the network and is available at most computer stores.

Jamming

Another threat, although not as common as eavesdropping, is jamming of a wireless network. Jamming involves using a transmitter to broadcast signals to a device or devices of a wireless network from a nearby location in an attempt to overload the wireless network and cause it to fail. Again, the equipment used to jam a wireless network is readily available. If you think you are experiencing jamming of your network, consult a networking or security specialist so they can determine the threat and offer solutions.

Reducing Threats

Nothing reduces the threats to a wireless network better than carefully planning your wireless network installation. Consult the documentation that comes with your wireless network equipment and fully implement any security measures that the hardware manufacturer recommends. If your network has particularly sensitive data on it, then it is best to consult with a network security specialist before implementing a wireless network.

The Newest
Network Security Specialists

Enable WEP Encryption

You can use Wired Equivalent Privacy (WEP) encryption to scramble the data transferred using a wireless network. This prevents unauthorized users from viewing information as it moves across your wireless network. The example in this section illustrates how to use a Web browser to configure a wireless device from Microsoft.

Remember to follow your wireless device instructions on opening the configuration settings for your device. For more information on setting up a wireless gateway and accessing the Base Station Management Tool screen, see Chapter 2.

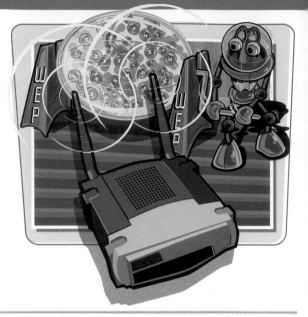

Enable WEP Encryption

① In the Base Station Management Tool screen, click **Security**.

② Click **Wireless Security**.

The Wireless Security screen appears.

③ Click the **Enable wireless security** option (○ changes to ◉).

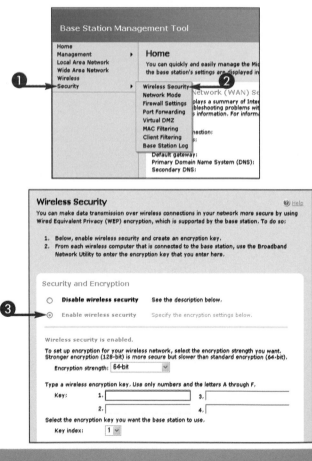

4 Click here and select an encryption strength.

This example uses the 128–bit (stronger) option.

Note: *Not all hardware allows you to create a security encryption key.*

Wireless Security ⚁ Help

You can make data transmission over wireless connections in your network more secure by using Wired Equivalent Privacy (WEP) encryption, which is supported by the base station. To do so:

1. Below, enable wireless security and create an encryption key.
2. From each wireless computer that is connected to the base station, use the Broadband Network Utility to enter the encryption key that you enter here.

Security and Encryption

○ **Disable wireless security** See the description below.

⊙ **Enable wireless security** Specify the encryption settings below.

Wireless security is enabled.

To set up encryption for your wireless network, select the encryption strength you want. Stronger encryption (128-bit) is more secure but slower than standard encryption (64-bit).

Encryption strength: 64-bit

128-bit (stronger)
64-bit

Type a wireless encrypti[on]   [numb]ers and the letters A through F.

Key: 1. [   ]   3. [   ]
         2. [   ]   4. [   ]

Select the encryption key you want the base station to use.

Key index: 1 ∨

5 Type a 26-digit encryption key using only letters A-F and numbers.

6 Click **Apply**.

Security and Encryption

○ **Disable wireless security** See the description below.

⊙ **Enable wireless security** Specify the encryption settings below.

Wireless security is enabled.

To set up encryption for your wireless network, select the encryption strength you want. Stronger encryption (128-bit) is more secure but slower than standard encryption (64-bit).

Encryption strength: 128-bit (stronger) ∨

Type a wireless encryption key. Use only numbers and the letters [A thro]ugh F.

Key: 1. [A123B456C789DA123B456C7]
         2. [   ]   4. [   ]

Select the encryption key you want the base station to use.

Key index: 1 ∨

[Apply] [Cancel]

 TIPS

What are the different encryption strengths and which should I select?

You can choose between 64-bit and 128-bit encryption. Use the highest encryption level your equipment allows. Keep in mind that your network may operate more slowly at the 128-bit setting because of the additional processing power the higher encryption level requires.

Can users easily access my computer from the Internet?

Although it is not necessarily easy to do, some users know how to exploit unprotected computers, such as those that do not use some form of encryption or firewall on their system. Assume that each time you connect to a network, including the Internet, someone has the possibility to access your computer. Take precautions against that.

continued

You can enable WEP encryption on your wireless network once the network is operating correctly. Make careful note of the WEP settings you choose. You cannot access the wireless network without them. Most small wireless networks do not use WEP to protect them. This is fine as long as the data and resources that are available are limited.

If you do not plan to use WEP, you should share only those folders that include nonsensitive information in them. Without WEP protection, do not share folders on wireless networks that include personnel files, private company information, trade secrets, and financial data.

Enable WEP Encryption *(continued)*

7 Right-click the Network Connection icon (🖳) in the system tray.

8 Click **Status**.

The Wireless Network Connection Status dialog box appears.

9 Click **Properties**.

The Wireless Network Connection Properties dialog box appears.

10 Click the **Wireless Networks** tab.

11 In the Preferred networks area, click **Properties**.

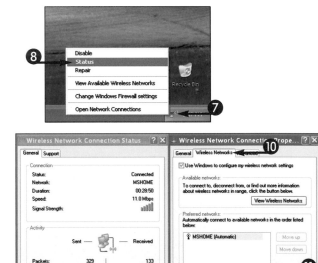

The properties dialog box for your network appears.

⑫ Click here and select **WEP** from the Data encryption list.

⑬ Type the key text generated in Step **5**.

⑭ Retype the key text.

⑮ Click **OK**.

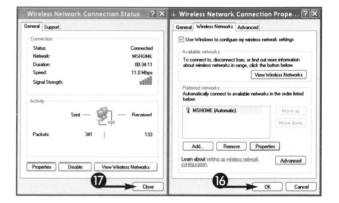

⑯ Click **OK** to close the Wireless Network Connection Properties dialog box.

⑰ Click **Close** to close the Wireless Network Connection Status dialog box.

The wireless network connection now uses WEP.

Change a Network Name

The SSID, or service set identifier, is the name used to identify your wireless network. When you initially configure a wireless network, you should change the SSID of the network to make it harder for unauthorized persons to access your wireless network.

The steps in this section show how to use a Web browser to configure a wireless router from Microsoft. Remember to follow your wireless device instructions on opening the configuration settings for your device.

① In the Base Station Management Tool screen, click **Wireless**.

The Wireless screen appears.

② Type a new name in the Wireless network name (SSID) field.

③ Click **Apply**.

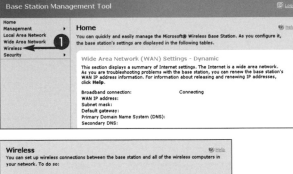

Windows displays a screen reminding you to configure each computer on your network with the new name.

4️⃣ Click **OK**.

Your router updates its settings.

Microsoft Internet Explorer

Remember, you must also configure each computer that connects wirelessly with the base station.

The base station and each computer that connects to it must use the same wireless network name and wireless channel number.

4️⃣ → ⟶ OK   Cancel

Wireless   ❷ Help

You can set up wireless connections between the base station and all of the wireless computers in your network. To do so:

1. Below, enter the wireless channel number, wireless network name (SSID), and data transmission rate you want to use.
2. From each wireless computer that you want to connect to the base station, use the Broadband Network Utility to enter the wireless network name that you enter here.

To make wireless data transmissions on your network more secure, set up wireless security (WEP).

☑ Enable wireless access

Wireless channel number: 6 ⌄

Wireless network name (SSID): MS_HOME

Data rate: auto ⌄

Apply   Cancel

Can I prevent others from viewing my SSID?

Yes, you may be able to prevent others from viewing your SSID. If your router provides a disabling feature, you can turn off SSID name broadcasting. Many routers provide this feature, but it means that all users connecting to your network must know the name, or SSID, of the wireless network.

Why should I need to change a network name?

In many cases you will not. However, if your network name matches another network in your area, you may want to change your network name to decrease confusion between the two networks. Also you may want to change the name if your company or organization changes names.

Manage a Hardware Access List

The MAC, or Media Access Control, address is a unique hardware identification number that every wireless device that connects to a wireless network must have. You can create a Hardware Access List that contains the MAC addresses of the network hardware that can connect to your wireless access point.

The steps in this section illustrate how to use a Web browser to configure a wireless router from Microsoft. Remember to follow your wireless device instructions on opening the configuration settings for your device.

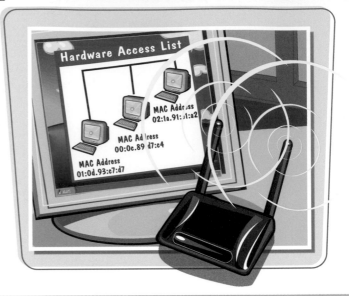

Manage a Hardware Access List

1 In the Base Station Management Tool screen, click **Wireless**.

Note: To access this screen as well as to learn more about setting up a wireless gateway, see Chapter 2.

2 Scroll down to the end of the screen.

3 Click **Refresh**.

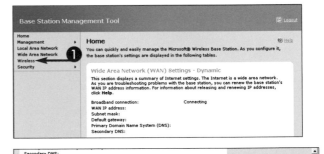

④ Scroll down to the end of the screen.

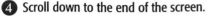

You see the updated information.

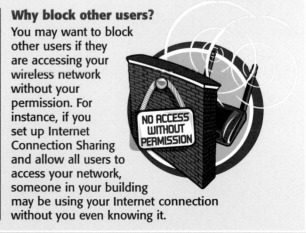

Can I prevent a specific wireless network from accessing my network?

If your router software lets you, you can block a specific piece of wireless networking hardware from connecting to your network by deleting its MAC address from the Access Control List. For example, you may want to block a MAC address that belongs to another person who uses the same wireless network as you, such as a neighbor.

Why block other users?

You may want to block other users if they are accessing your wireless network without your permission. For instance, if you set up Internet Connection Sharing and allow all users to access your network, someone in your building may be using your Internet connection without you even knowing it.

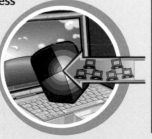

Configure Windows Firewall

You can install firewall software that prevents unauthorized Internet traffic from entering or leaving the computers on your network. A firewall prevents unauthorized users from gaining access to your wireless network. Windows Firewall is one of the most used firewall applications and is available with Windows XP.

The basic way a firewall works is by masking the true identity of the computers on your network. The firewall becomes a "proxy" for your computer to the outside world (the Internet). Users on the Internet can see the firewall address, but cannot see behind it to view individual computers on the network.

Configure Windows Firewall

① Click **start**.

② Click **Control Panel**.

The Control Panel window appears.

③ Click the **Network and Internet Connections** icon ( ).

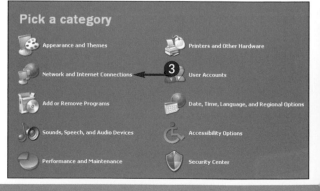

The Network and Internet Connections window appears.

④ Click **Windows Firewall**.

The Windows Firewall dialog box appears.

⑤ Click the **On (recommended)** option (○ changes to ⊙).

Windows Firewall turns on.

⑥ Click **OK**.

Windows Firewall is enabled.

 TIPS

Where can I find a good firewall?

There are many other firewall products available, including some that are free. You can download firewall software from Sunbelt Software, which offers home users a free version of Sunbelt Kerio Personal Firewall at www.sunbelt-software.com/Kerio.cfm.

Do firewalls keep all intruders out?

No. Some intruders can gain access to your system even if you put up a firewall. However, firewalls offer one of the best defenses to keeping out potentially harmful intruders.

Manage Windows Firewall

Windows Firewall blocks users trying to access your computer using Windows Remote Desktop. Your wireless gateway probably has a built-in firewall, but it may be limited in its features.

Windows Firewall enables you to set up exceptions, which lets you turn on the firewall for all but those programs and services you want to allow access to your computer. This is handy when you know the firewall blocks programs and services that you want to use, such as file and printer sharing.

Manage Windows Firewall

① Start the Windows Firewall application.

Note: See the section "Configure Windows Firewall" to open the Windows Firewall dialog box.

② Click the **Don't allow exceptions** option (☐ changes to ☑).

③ Click the **Exceptions** tab.

④ Click the **Remote Desktop** option (☐ changes to ☑).

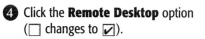

5 Deselect the **File and Printer Sharing** option (☐ changes to ☑).

6 Click the **Display a notification when Windows Firewall blocks a program** option (☐ changes to ☑).

7 Click **OK**.

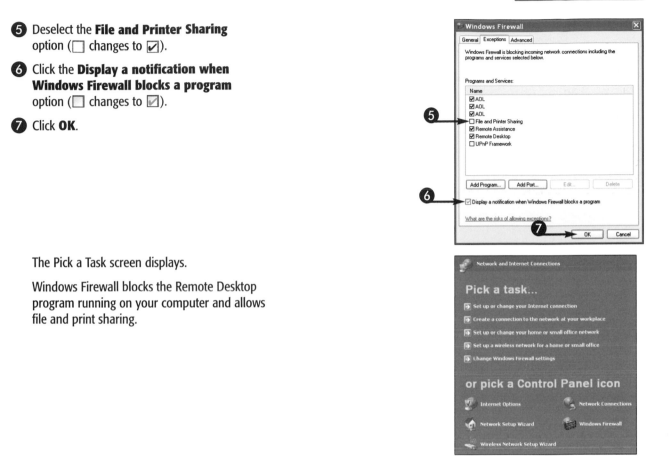

The Pick a Task screen displays.

Windows Firewall blocks the Remote Desktop program running on your computer and allows file and print sharing.

TIPS

How do I troubleshoot problems with the firewall?

Windows Firewall includes a log file tool that helps you troubleshoot problems. Turn it on by opening the Windows Firewall program. Click the **Advanced** tab and click **Settings** under the Security Login area. Click the **Log dropped packets option** (○ changes to ◉). Click **OK**, and then click **OK** again.

Does Windows detect every kind of firewall?

No. Windows cannot detect all firewalls available on the market. Make sure that the one you purchase or download works with Windows XP (or the operating system you use).

Disable Windows Firewall

Windows Firewall is easy to use and offers a tremendous amount of control over the programs and services that run on your computer across a wireless network. The disadvantage of Windows Firewall is that it can block too much traffic, sometimes rendering your network and Internet connections worthless. You may want to disable Windows Firewall to allow you to work on the network.

A good time to disable Windows Firewall is after you install a network or Internet program and the program does not operate correctly. Temporarily disable Windows Firewall and test the program again. If it works fine, Windows Firewall may need to be set to allow that program to operate.

Disable Windows Firewall

① Click **start**.

② Click **Control Panel**.

The Control Panel window appears.

③ Click ▣.

The Network and Internet Connections window appears.

④ Click .

The Windows Firewall dialog box appears.

⑤ Click the **Off (not recommended)** option (◯ changes to ◉).

Windows Firewall turns off.

⑥ Click **OK**.

Windows Firewall is disabled.

TIPS

What should I do to keep intruders out of my network?

Windows Firewall is not a cure-all to all the problems you may encounter with unauthorized programs and services running on your computer. You must follow good network protection procedures to protect yourself. This includes using a strong password, monitoring users who have access to your computer, and keeping the number of shared folders to a minimum.

Does Microsoft update Windows Firewall?

Yes. Microsoft has in the past made available updates to Windows Firewall. To find out more about Windows Firewall, visit the Web at www.microsoft.com/windows/firewall.

Connecting on the Road

Laptop computers are popular because you can carry them with you to almost any destination. This popularity means businesses, hotels, schools, and metropolitan areas are providing more public access to wireless networks. This chapter shows you how to connect your laptop computer to wireless networks when you travel so you can access the Internet or an office network. It also shows you how to connect to Wi-Fi networks in airports, coffee shops, and other public areas.

Discover the Benefits of a Mobile Computer

A mobile computer enables you to take advantage of the wireless networks that are popping up in offices, homes, hotels, coffee shops, and metropolitan areas. Mobile computers provide an easy way to move around without being tied to a desk.

Work Out Solutions

With a mobile computer, you can move to a different office, room, building, or country, and still perform your job. For example, if you have an important Monday morning deadline that requires you to work extra time over a weekend, instead of driving into work, you can simply load up the work on your laptop, take the laptop with you over the weekend, and finish your work.

Provide Sharing of Resources

You can share a mobile computer amongst workers. Many organizations purchase loaner laptops that employees can borrow for business trips, meetings, and personal use. One way these shared resources benefit the employee is for presentations. With a loaner laptop, employees can load up a presentation or download one from a shared network drive, move to a presentation room, and display the presentation over a projector. For more about giving presentations, see Chapter 8.

Access to Wireless Resources

Of course the main reason you want a mobile computer is so you can access the large number of wireless resources in your area. Wireless resources are the networks and services provided by those services. For example, one common network resource is shared printing. With a shared printer, a wireless network can have several users print to the same device. This decreases the overall cost of computing because you only need to purchase, update, and maintain one printer.

Freedom to Travel

When you travel you can look for and use wireless access points to connect to the Internet, communicate with other users, share files, and send and receive e-mail messages. You can also use your computer to entertain yourself while you are on the road. For more on communicating using your wireless computer, see Chapter 7. For more on sharing files, see Chapter 5. For more on using your computer as a source of entertainment, see Chapter 9.

A Way to Work as Groups

With a mobile computer and wireless networking, you can create ad-hoc groups in your company, organization, or family. These groups can then work on group solutions to problems, communicate with each other, or gather together to share games and other entertainment features.

Buying a Mobile Computer

Before dashing out and purchasing a computer, there are some considerations you may want to review. The following are some general buying tips you can follow before you go out shopping.

Know Your Requirements

Assess the different types of jobs you need to do with your mobile computer. For example, do you use a computer mainly for connecting to the Internet to download, read, and reply to e-mail? Do you take digital photographs and want to view and edit those while you travel? Maybe you need just a Web browser. When you know what you need, write down the minimum system resources for these programs.

Know Your Office's Requirements

After you determine what you need for yourself, understand what your work requires. Your office may have specific applications that you must use to create text documents, present proposals, submit travel requests, and time tracking. Do you need productivity software, such as word processors, spreadsheets, and database programs? Again, when you know what you need, write down the minimum system resources for these programs.

Price versus Features

As you begin to consider the type of mobile computer you want to purchase, think about price. Some laptops cost as little as $299, while others can top above $2000. When purchasing a mobile computer, higher price usually correlates to faster processing speeds, higher and faster memory, more disk space, lighter weight, and other benefits. However, if all you want — and need — is a mobile computer with the basics, a mobile computer in the lower price range will probably suffice.

Price versus Performance

Today's typical laptop computer, regardless of price, usually has enough processor power and memory to support most everyday applications. If you want to have the most powerful and fastest high-performance laptop on the market, however, you have to pay a premium price.

Warranty Considerations

Laptops, by nature, have parts that can break, and leave you unproductive. Before you purchase a laptop, always make sure that you check out the warranty. Does the manufacturer have a good record of helping you resolve problems? Are they easy to contact? Can you get through to an actual person in case of emergency?

Discover Value-Priced Laptop Computers

Low price does not always mean low quality. When you decide to purchase a mobile computer, start at the bottom and work your way up. Look at the features listed here to help you make your decision on purchasing a lower-priced laptop computer for your wireless networking needs. These laptops are generally in the $299-$999 range.

Processor

Many of your lower priced laptops include the Intel Celeron processor. Celeron processors are less expensive alternatives to the more popular and higher rated Intel Pentium or Intel Centrino mobile processor. Celeron processors are excellent for everyday usage and are extremely reliable for the average mobile user. In most cases, when you use your mobile computer for spreadsheet use, word processing, Web browsing, and e-mail, a Celeron processor is all you need.

Laptop Weight

Laptops come in a variety of weights. For a budget-minded shopper, you will probably not find a laptop that weighs below 6 pounds. Typically a laptop that falls in the below $1000 range weighs between 6 and 10 pounds.

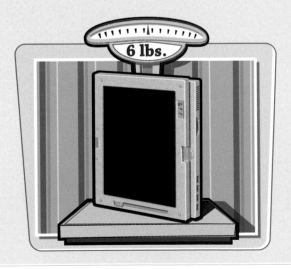

Travel Weight

One thing to remember when you are concerned about laptop weight is the actual travel weight of your mobile computer. This includes things like extra batteries, extra power supplies, backup CDs, and external storage devices. If you can live with a 10-pound mobile computer, know that you will probably add another 10 pounds of accessories that becomes your traveling weight.

Screen Size

The screen size of a typical laptop computer is not designed to replace the larger monitors that desktop computers have. However, screen sizes for laptops have gone from 9 inches just 10 years ago to over 19 inches now. For lower-priced laptops, however, you will probably find screen sizes in the 14.5" to 17" range. Screens that are 17" or larger are termed *wide-screen monitors*. This is because the screens are wider than they are tall, allowing you to view wider objects on screen a lot easier. One application that takes real advantage of wide-screen technology is spreadsheet application. This is because many spreadsheets include several columns of data that extend past the right edge of a narrower screen.

Storage Options

Even by storing critical data and information on a wireless network drive, you still need built-in storage for your lower-priced laptop. Your programs, permanent data, and many other types of files need to reside on an internal hard drive. Value-priced laptops typically have hard drive capacities of 40-80GB, usually on the lower end as your prices get closer to the $299 range. You also can purchase an external storage device, such as an 120GB external hard drive, if your internal hard drive fills up too quickly. Make sure you consider the weight of the external drive as you calculate your traveling weight.

Discover High-Quality Laptop Computers

Everyone usually wants the best of anything. We all want the biggest, fastest, best performing, and best looking car on the market. If we travel with our computers, we want the same as well. But you need to consider the following factors as you look into purchasing a high quality laptop computer. These laptops are generally in the $1000 to $3000 range.

Top of the Line Laptop

For the serious computer enthusiast

$$$$$

Processor

When you need the highest quality processor for wireless networking and mobile work, consider a computer equipped with the Intel Centrino mobile processor. This processor is optimized for use in laptops. It provides efficient power usage, extends the life of batteries, and provides more processing power in a smaller package. The latter point enables laptops to be built smaller and lighter.

Weight

Mobile computers that are higher priced are usually in the thin and light category. Thin means the laptop is thinner than lower-priced, heavier computers. Some high priced thin models are less than 1" in thickness. The light category includes computers that weigh less than 6 pounds. Some weigh as low as 4 pounds or less. If you travel all the time and do not want to lug around a 10 pound mobile computer — and you can afford it — consider a thin and light computer.

Storage Options

Mobile computers built to be light weight — under 6 pounds — do not have all the hardware features of your heavier models. Typically these do not have some of the built-in features, such as internal CD-R/DVD drives. For the times you need to access a CD-R/DVD drive, you must connect a portable one to your computer. Another option for storage is flash drives. These are typically small devices you can carry in your pocket. They plug directly into a USB port on your computer and can store a large amount of data, over 2GB in some cases. Finally, external hard drives come in packages that are easy to carry and connect. Some of these can hold over 120GB of data.

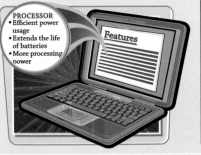

PROCESSOR
• Efficient power usage
• Extends the life of batteries
• More processing power

Features

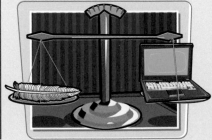

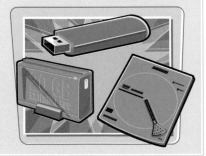

Your mobile computer must use a power source to run. Two types of power sources are available: battery and AC power. AC power involves using a power cord and a transformer that connects your computer to a standard electrical outlet. When you cannot connect to an outlet, you use a battery.

Types of Batteries

The type of battery your laptop uses greatly affects its life, how long it can hold a charge, and its recharge rate. Typically laptop batteries use either Nickel Metal Hydride (NiMH) or Lithium Ion (Li-ION) technologies. Typically Lithium Ion hold charges longer than NiMH battery. Lithium Ion batteries can hold charges for over 4 hours, while NiMH are typically 2 1/2 hours. Li-Ion batteries are also lighter in weight than NiMH batteries. The downside to Li-Ion batteries is that they usually have shorter life-spans than other batteries.

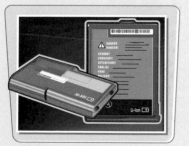

Recharge Batteries

You must recharge any laptop battery to replenish it with power. As you use your computer in mobile situations, such as working in a sidewalk café, an airport terminal, or outside on your company's deck, the battery slowly drains. To recharge the battery, simply plug in the laptops power cord to an AC outlet. Over a period of time, depending on the type of battery you have, the make of your computer, and other factors, the battery will recharge. You can then unplug the power cord and return to your mobile computing.

Additional Power Supplies

To aid in recharging and powering your mobile computer, consider purchasing multiple power supplies. This enables you to have power supplies in the most convenient locations for you. For example, if you carry your laptop into work everyday, consider a second power supply for your main office that you can leave plugged in. When you come into work, unpack your laptop, plug in the power cord, and start working. With multiple power cords, you also can keep a power supply in your laptop case so when you travel you always have one available for power and for recharging the battery.

Connect Away from Home

Public locations that provide wireless network access allow you to use your mobile computer. As more and more users and workers rely on mobile technologies, wireless networks will grow and become more prevalent. In some metropolitan areas, for example, wireless networks are available to any person who has a computer and a wireless network card.

Large hotel chains, shopping malls, and many restaurants have access to wireless networking resources. For example, some restaurant chains sell networking time just like they do a cup of coffee.

WIRELESS INTERNET AVAILABLE

Internet Access

The primary purpose of connecting to a wireless network in a public location is to gain Internet access. Once a mobile device has Internet access, the user is free to use the mobile device for applications that allow people to communicate, such as sending and receiving e-mail messages.

Reminder!
Meeting @ 7pm
Wednesday night!

Socializing

You can also use wireless networks for nonbusiness reasons, such as using the wireless network to meet and communicate with others. Just like chat rooms and other communications forums on the Internet, you can easily communicate with other users on the wireless network to which you are attached.

Network Connections

Public wireless networks also allow a user to form a connection with another computer connected to the Internet using a secure connection called a virtual private network (VPN). A VPN allows users to access information stored on computers and networks located at their home, or more commonly, at work.

Hotspots

A *hotspot* is the name given to a location that has wireless network access. The hotspot may be limited to a single room, such as the lounge in a hotel, or it can be much larger, such as within city limits.

Service Providers

Many companies provide wireless access. Wireless service providers install the necessary hardware that provides coverage to the location such as a café or airport. Most installations are permanent, but some are temporary, such as wireless networks provided for clients of trade shows or conferences. More than one provider may serve a single location.

Wireless Service Providers

Due to better standards, cheaper hardware, faster connection times, and lower access fees, many companies now provide wireless network access to locations around the world. To connect to a service provider, you must install software or modify your existing wireless network settings to ensure your computer is set up with the same protocols, a network name, and a proper username.

Before leaving on business trips, many companies now require their workers to learn about wireless networks in the area they plan to visit. This provides them with a means to communicate with the office while away.

Standards

Wireless services most commonly use a wireless standard referred to as 802.11b, which provides network speeds of 11 Mbps. Some locations also use the 802.11g standard, which has speeds of up to 54 Mbps. Most wireless network adapters work with the wireless standards used at hotspots.

Cost

Most wireless networks require you to pay a fee to access the network. Some service providers require you to pay a fee up front, while other locations may allow you to use the wireless network to purchase or use a product purchased from the location where you use the service.

Configuration

Some service providers may require that you use their custom connection software to connect to their wireless networks. Most wireless service providers allow you to connect to their wireless network by entering the correct name of the wireless network into the configuration of your wireless network adapter on your mobile computer.

Hardware

Most service providers allow you to connect with a laptop, which has a wireless network adapter, as well as with a handheld computer. Typically, you have restrictions as to the operating system you use on the mobile device. Some networks may not allow access using handheld computers.

Roaming

Roaming is the ability to sign up as a client of one service provider and use the services of another service provider, which gives the user more wireless network hotspots without signing up with numerous providers. Unlike mobile telephone providers, wireless access service providers cannot give you comprehensive roaming services, but they may in the future.

Find Wi-Fi Hotspots

A *hotspot* is a public wireless network access point. Although more and more are becoming available, not all hotspots use the same settings and names. You can find wireless networks using a hotspot directory. For example, the Wi-Fi Alliance, an industry trade group, maintains the Wi-Fi Zone Finder Web site, a directory of wireless network providers and their locations.

Before you head to a new city, use the Wi-Fi Zone Finder Web site to locate Wi-Fi zones. This way you can map out where you are most likely to connect to a wireless network when you arrive at your destination.

Find Wi-Fi Hotspots

① Open your Web browser and type **http://wi-fi.jiwire.com/** in the Address field.

The Wi-Fi Zone Finder home page appears.

② Scroll down to the middle of the page.

③ Type the name of the city you want to search.

④ Click here and select a location type.

This example searches for Wi-Fi hotspots in Chicago airports.

⑤ Click **Go**.

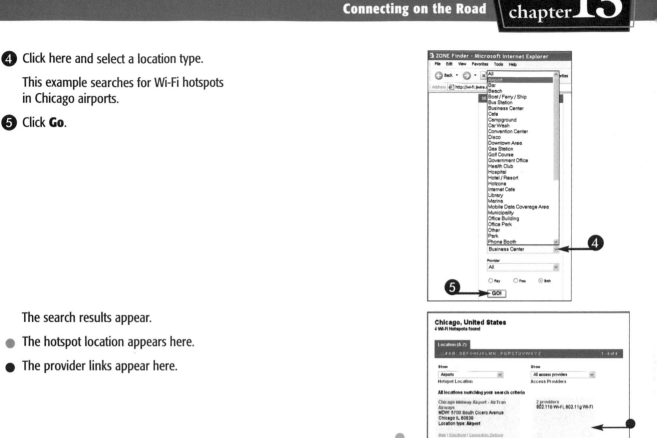

The search results appear.

● The hotspot location appears here.

● The provider links appear here.

TIPS

How do I find Wi-Fi resources?

You can use an Internet search engine, such as Google, to find the latest Wi-Fi directory resources. To do this, open your Web browser and type **www.google.com**. In the Google search field, type **Wi-Fi hotspots**. The Google search results page appears with a list of links to Wi-Fi hotspot sites.

Why do some Wi-Fi hotspots disappear?

Wi-Fi hotspots can disappear if a network problem occurs, the access point is shut down — such as for routine maintenance — or if the network experiences an overwhelming number of users. Usually if you get knocked off the network, try again later to see if the connection is back up.

View Available Networks

When you travel, your laptop computer, or other Wi-Fi-compatible device, identifies wireless networks that are broadcasting their presence. Your computer displays a list of these available networks, and you can connect to one of them.

Keep in mind that hotspots come and go. A spot you linked to last month may not be available this month. This is why a Web site like the Wi-Fi Zone is so handy. It does a great job of keeping track of those newer hotspots that you may not be familiar with yet.

View Available Networks

① Right-click the **Network Connection** icon (⬚).

② Click **View Available Wireless Networks**.

The Wireless Network Connection window appears.

③ Click an available network.

④ Click **Connect**.

● The status of the network changes to Connected.

5 Click the **Close** icon (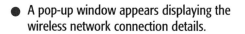).

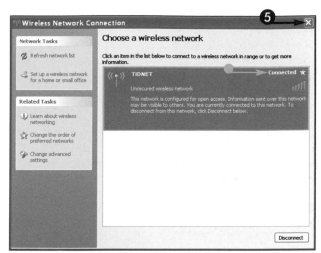

● A pop-up window appears displaying the wireless network connection details.

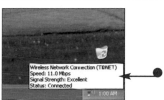

TIPS

What Wi-Fi providers are out there for me to access?

There are national Wi-Fi network access providers you can connect to, such as Boingo Wireless. You can find more information about Boingo Wireless at www.boingo.com. You can also go to a search engine, such as Google, and type **national Wi-Fi provider** in the search field to display a list of other providers.

My city has Wi-Fi for everyone. How do I access it?

That depends on how it is set up. If they require you to have an account, contact your city building for access information. If an account is not required, use Windows' Zero Configuration service to allow it to search for all available networks, including your city's hotspot. For more on configuring Zero Configuration, see Chapter 4.

Set Up a VPN Connection

You can access your corporate network using a *virtual private network* (VPN) connection. A VPN creates a safe connection between your computer and a VPN server by securely connecting through your wireless network and the Internet.

Many corporations use VPNs so that computers that are not permanently connected to their network can gain access to their networks in a secure way. Although you can use a dial-up modem, VPNs replace standard dial-up connectivity, which may become a security problem for many networks. Companies can use strict security measures to protect VPN connections.

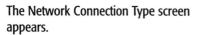

Set Up a VPN Connection

① From the Network Connections window, click the **Create a new connection** link.

The New Connection Wizard appears.

② Click **Next**.

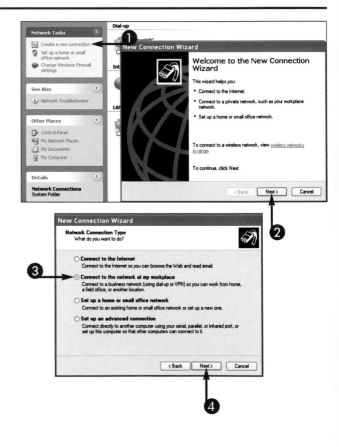

The Network Connection Type screen appears.

③ Click the **Connect to the network at my workplace** option (○ changes to ◉).

④ Click Next.

The Network Connection screen appears.

⑤ Click the **Virtual Private Network connection** option (○ changes to ◉).

⑥ Click **Next**.

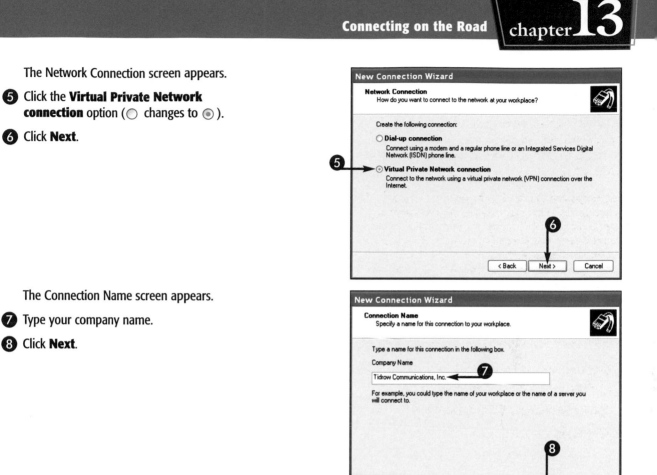

The Connection Name screen appears.

⑦ Type your company name.

⑧ Click **Next**.

 TIPS

Can my computer receive VPN connections?

Yes, your computer also can accept incoming VPN connections. You can enable incoming VPN connections with the New Connection Wizard. Other users on your wireless network can then use a VPN connection to connect securely to your computer.

Why should I use a VPN and not a dial-up connection?

One big advantage is cost savings for those who normally have to access the company through a long-distance telephone call. A VPN connection uses the Internet so users just need to connect to the Internet locally — such as through a local phone call or broadband connection — and then connect to the company VPN.

continued

You can connect to your VPN server while traveling, which enables you to access information on your work computer from your mobile computer. One main use of VPN connections is access to corporate-wide e-mail servers. While users are out of the office, such as on business trips or vacation, they can still connect to the VPN server and access their e-mail and calendar.

Another tool that VPNs take advantage of is the Windows Remote Desktop application. With a VPN connection, users can access their desktop computer via a remote login through the VPN.

Set Up a VPN Connection *(continued)*

The Public Network screen appears.

9 Click the **Do not dial the initial connection** option (○ changes to ◉).

10 Click **Next**.

The VPN Server Selection screen appears.

11 Type the name of your VPN host.

12 Click **Next**.

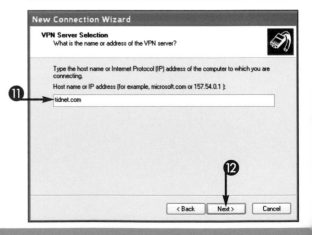

The Completing the New Connection Wizard screen appears.

⑬ Click **Finish**.

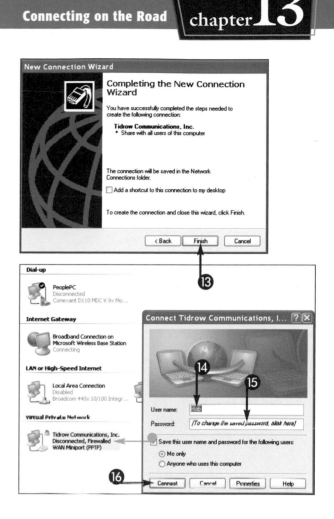

The Connect dialog box appears.

⑭ Type your username.

⑮ Type your password.

⑯ Click **Connect**.

● Your computer creates a secure connection with your VPN server.

How do I disconnect a VPN connection?

You can disconnect a VPN connection by right-clicking the VPN connection icon and selecting **Disconnect**.

Do all companies use VPN connections?

No. Some companies do not use VPNs because they do not want outside users, including employees, to access the Internal network. In addition, some companies do not find it a cost-effective benefit to offer VPN access for their company resources. VPNs do increase overhead in terms of hardware resources, security, and administration time.

Improving Network Performance

You can increase the speed and improve the reliability of your wireless network by making a few basic changes. This chapter tells you how you can improve signal range and strength, as well as how to use monitoring software.

Understanding Factors Affecting Wireless Range

The range of a network is the geographic distance that a network can comprise. The shorter the range is, the smaller the distance between the wireless devices. Many factors affect the signal range and quality of your wireless network.

Hardware Location

To ensure that you are within receiving range, place your access points to within 150 feet of the computers on your network. You can increase the range by using switched access points. These types of access points do not have all the features of regular access points, but can allow you to create a daisy chain of access points to extend your wireless network range.

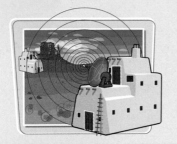

Physical Environment

Wireless network signals travel farther in open areas, such as outdoors or in an office with few walls. Metal, concrete, and brick reduce the distance that radio signals can travel. If possible, move transmitters and receivers to outdoor areas, such as rooftops, overhangs, television towers, and signs. If you are transmitting signals from one building to another, you should always place your transmitter and receiver outside. Attempt to line up the two devices to each other, also, thereby reducing how much the signal will spread.

Nearby Signals

Cordless telephones, microwave ovens, security cameras, security systems, and X-10 gear, which is used mainly in home automation devices, emit radio signals that can interfere with many Wi-Fi networks. These devices can reduce and degrade the strength and quality of your network signal. If you are in an area that has a great deal of radio signal interference, your best bet is to go with a hybrid network. Use wireless devices in areas in which the interfering signals are the weakest. For the places where the interference is the greatest, use wired solutions. This may mean that you have to run some network cable from one building to the next in order to maintain your network.

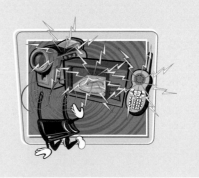

Increase Wireless Range

Improving Network Performance

chapter **14**

You can increase the range and quality of your wireless network by changing the location of your equipment, reducing interference from other transmitters, and adjusting the antennas on your network adapters and access points.

Move Access Points

You can increase the range of your network by placing your wireless access point in an elevated place. You can also move your access point to the center of your network. By moving it to the center, you give all surrounding computers equal share of the wireless signal as it emits from the transmitter. One way many companies expand the range of their Wi-Fi network is to mount access points on the ceilings of the buildings. This eliminates interferences caused by printers, desks, cubicle walls, furniture, and other items located on the floor.

Reduce Interference

You can reduce interference by moving your wireless access points away from cordless telephones, microwave ovens, and computers. You can also move access points away from large metal surfaces. Another cause of interference is having two similar devices too close together. For example, if you have one access point device set up too close to another one, they both may cancel each other's signals. Move one of them to a different location so that their signals do not overlap too much. To determine how far you can move each device, consult the device's documentation for maximum placement distances. For example, some devices cannot exceed 130 feet between them to remain at their maximum effectiveness.

Adjust Antennas

Make sure your wireless antennas are secured tightly to your equipment in an upright position. However, you may find that your signal strength increases if you move the antenna position. Experiment with the antenna at different angles until your mobile computers get the best reception. Also, if your mobile and desktop computers use a wireless network card that has an attached antenna, position it at different angles to get the optimum reception as well.

The strength of the wireless radio signal has a direct influence on the speed of communication on the network as well as how far apart the wireless network device can be. You can monitor the strength of your wireless network with a software program called NetStumbler, also called Network Stumbler.

Monitor Radio Signals

① Open your Web browser and type **www.netstumbler.com** in the Address field.

The NetStumbler home page appears.

② Click the **Downloads** link.

The Downloads page appears.

③ Click the **NetStumbler 0.4.0 Installer** download link.

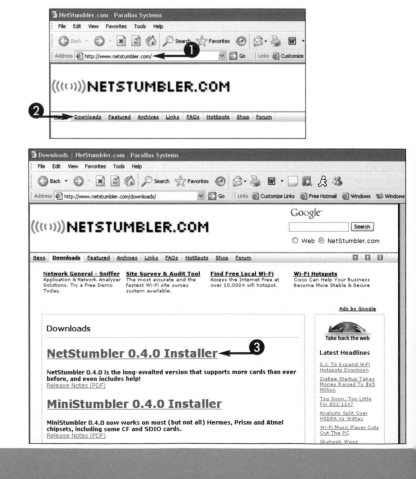

The File Download – Security Warning appears.

④ Click **Save**.

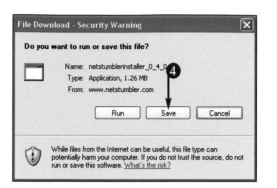

The Save As dialog box appears.

⑤ Click **Save**.

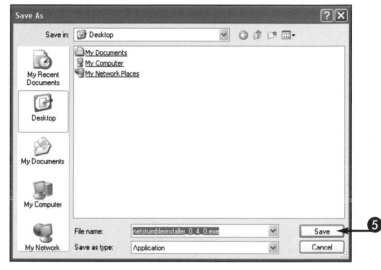

continued

TIPS

Do I have to pay for NetStumbler?

NetStumbler is free for personal use; however, the developer may charge businesses and institutions for their use of this software. If you are in a corporation, consult your manager or information technology director for information on installing NetStumbler on your company computer.

Is NetStumbler the only software for this kind of job?

No. There are several others, including MiniStumbler, a smaller version of NetStumble, available from the NetStumbler downloads page. Other programs that are network sniffers for wireless networks include Ethereal Network Analyzer and IP Sniffer.

You can measure the radio strength of nearby wireless devices that you can connect to with your computer. If the radio strength is adequate and you have the appropriate authorization, you can then connect to the wireless device.

Monitor Radio Signals (continued)

The installation file downloads and appears on your desktop.

6 Double-click the installation icon.

The Network Stumbler Setup: License Agreement page appears.

7 Click **I Agree**.

The Network Stumbler Setup: Choose Components page appears.

8 Click **Next**.

The Network Stumbler Setup Choose Install Location page appears.

9 Click **Install**.

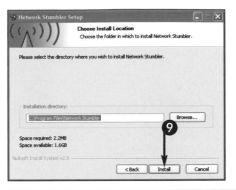

Network Stumbler installs on your computer.

● A Network Stumbler program icon appears on your desktop.

10 Click **Close**.

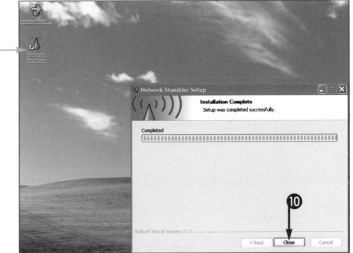

TIPS

Are there other ways I can use NetStumbler?

You can use NetStumbler to determine if others can see your wireless network. You also can walk outside your residence or business with a laptop computer and use NetStumbler to see how far your network reaches.

What is a packet sniffer?

Packet sniffer is a name used to describe network protocol analyzers. These analyzers look over networks and find network signals, IP traffic, filters, and other network settings. Essentially they sniff out network data packets, hence the name packet sniffer.

continued

NetStumbler measures the signal strength-to-noise ratio of your wireless network in decibels. Higher decibel levels indicate stronger signals; the stronger the signal, the faster you can transfer information over the network.

Monitor Radio Signals *(continued)*

A help window appears, showing NetStumbler Help.

⑪ Click the Close icon (☒).

The NetStumbler Help window closes.

⑫ Double-click the application icon.

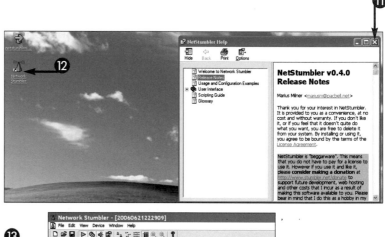

The Network Stumbler window appears.

⑬ Click the plus sign (⊞) next to Channels (⊞ changes to ⊟).

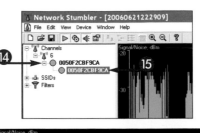

⑭ Click ⊞ again until you reach an active SSID (⊞ changes to ⊟).

Note: *For more information service set identifiers (SSID), see Chapter 4.*

⑮ Click the MAC hardware address.

The Network Stumbler real-time monitoring page appears.

● The signal should transmit perfectly.

● The signal transmission is good.

● The signal transmission is most likely poor.

Extremely poor signal transmission will result in a significant loss of data packets.

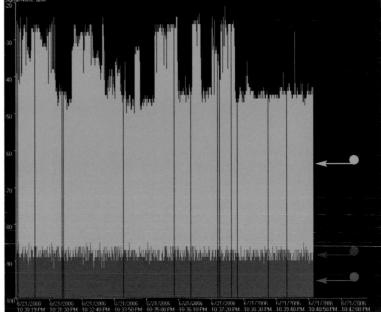

TIPS

Where can I get NetStumbler?

The NetStumbler application is available for download, with additional information about using the application, at www.netstumbler. com.

www.netstumbler.com

Can I use Network Stumbler for more than one access point?

Yes. When you click the plus signs (⊞) next to each channel or SSID, you see a list of all the SSIDs available. If there are multiple access points, there will be multiple SSIDs listed. Examine one or all access points that Network Stumbler lists.

CHAPTER 15

Troubleshooting a Wireless Network

You may occasionally need to troubleshoot problems that arise with your wireless network. In this chapter, you will learn how to use the Network Diagnostics tool and other network utilities to help you solve these problems.

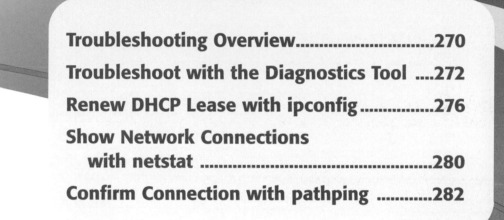

Troubleshooting Overview

When problems arise on a wireless network, you can use the same techniques and tools for traditional cable networks to troubleshoot.

Service Professionals

Because most problems with wireless networks are relatively simple, you can resolve them without outside help. Unfortunately, some problems, especially those related to security, require the assistance of trained and skilled computer professionals. Never hesitate to call a professional if you think your problems may be security related.

Network Tools

You can use many network tools to determine the cause and the resolution of wireless network problems. Network hardware often come with monitoring tools to view the performance on the wireless network, while applications exist that will allow you to closely inspect all the information on a network.

Documentation

One of the most neglected tools available for troubleshooting a wireless network is the documentation that came with the wireless network hardware. To ensure your network hardware is correctly configured and installed, always review the network hardware documentation thoroughly when troubleshooting network problems. For example, repositioning an antenna using the manufacturer's guidelines may increase the efficiency of the network substantially.

Process of Elimination

As with many computer-related problems, determining the cause of a problem in a wireless network is a process of elimination. For example, if something is causing the network speed to slow down, turn on each device and computer and start each network application one at a time until the problem occurs. This may allow you to pinpoint the cause of the problem. Continue this process to include other devices that operate on the same radio spectrum or cause noise in the wireless spectrum. These devices include 2.4 Ghz cordless phones, wireless alarm system components, microwave ovens, and remote extenders.

Unique to Wireless

The problems experienced on wireless networks are typically the same problems experienced by other cable networks. Problems unique to wireless networks are limited to hardware problems, such as faulty antennas or the incorrect placement of access points. The fastest way to determine if there is a problem with network hardware is to substitute the hardware for hardware that works.

Troubleshoot with the Diagnostics Tool

You can use the Windows XP Network Diagnostics troubleshooting tool to help you determine why your network is not working properly, as well as to diagnose other network problems. This built-in tool can automatically run networking tests, which saves you time.

Troubleshoot with the Diagnostics Tool

① Click **start**.

② Click **Control Panel**.

The Control Panel window appears.

③ Click **Network and Internet Connections** icon (■).

The Network and Internet Connections window appears.

4 Click the **Network Diagnostics** link.

The Help and Support Center window appears.

5 Click the **Scan your system** link.

When I scan my system, can I choose which tests to perform?

Yes. You can click the **Set scanning options** link in the Help and Support Center window to select the actions and categories you want Network Diagnostics to scan. You can decrease the scanning time by deselecting unnecessary options (☐ changes to ☑).

How long does the network diagnostics run?

The time depends on how quickly each network device, service, and application reports findings back to Network Diagnostics. Usually if there are problems with network connections, the Network Diagnostics tool can take several minutes to determine if the signal is bad or just weak.

continued

In many cases, the Network Diagnostics tool can point out problems that you or your network administrator can solve. The Network Diagnostics tool should be the first step in troubleshooting wireless connection problems.

Not only does the Network Diagnostics tool report information about hardware, but it also reports information about network applications. These types of applications include e-mail programs, the operating system (Windows itself), and Internet Explorer.

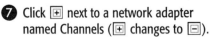

Troubleshoot with the Diagnostics Tool *(continued)*

The Network Diagnostics tool scans the network components you specify.

The Network Diagnostics tool displays the scan results.

6 Click the ⊞ for **Network Adapters** (⊞ changes to ⊟).

Additional details about failed tests appear.

7 Click ⊞ next to a network adapter named Channels (⊞ changes to ⊟).

● Additional details about the tests done on the network adapter appear.

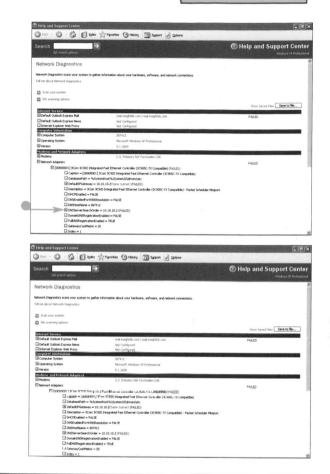

You can use the information from the failed tests to help you or your network administrator to solve the problem.

TIPS

What should I do before using network-troubleshooting utilities?

You should turn off any firewall software that you have running on the computers you are troubleshooting. For more information about firewall software, see Chapter 12. You should also install the newest software drivers for your network adapters. To update network adapter drivers, see Chapters 2 and 3.

How can this information help me fix my problem?

The primary way it can help you is by pointing out devices, programs, and services that have failed. When you see which ones have failed, you can focus your attention on those areas, instead of in areas that do not appear to be problematic. Another way you can fix your networking problem through a diagnostic tool is by reporting the results to a networking specialist. Specialists can quickly read the information returned by the diagnostic tool and advise you on how to correct the problems.

Renew DHCP Lease with ipconfig

You can use the ipconfig utility to restore the connection between your computer and your wireless network. ipconfig is a Windows XP utility that you can run from the Command Prompt window. The Command Prompt is a built-in part of Windows where you run tools, services, and programs by typing in commands.

Although many users will shy away from the Command Prompt — they may feel it is too intimidating — the commands you learn here are easy to use, do not harm the computer, and are useful in many situations. You should make it a point to understand how to use this and other Command Prompt tools.

Renew DHCP Lease with ipconfig

① Click **start**.

② Click **All Programs**.

③ Click **Accessories**.

④ Click **Command Prompt**.

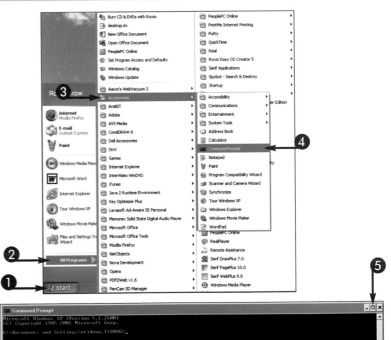

The Command Prompt window appears.

⑤ Click the **Maximize** icon (□).

The Command Prompt window fills the screen.

6 Type **ipconfig /release**.

7 Press **Enter**.

```
Command Prompt
Microsoft Windows XP [Version 5.1.2600]
(C) Copyright 1985-2001 Microsoft Corp.

C:\Documents and Settings\rtidrow.TIDROW>ipconfig /release      6
```

The Command Prompt window displays the Windows IP Configuration results.

● If the utility successfully renews your DHCP lease, the results show an IP Address of 0.0.0.0.

● If the Command Prompt window does not show an IP Address of 0.0.0.0, repeat Steps **1** to **7** before continuing.

```
Command Prompt
Microsoft Windows XP [Version 5.1.2600]
(C) Copyright 1985-2001 Microsoft Corp.

C:\Documents and Settings\rtidrow.TIDROW>ipconfig /release

Windows IP Configuration

Ethernet adapter Local Area Connection 3:

        Connection-specific DNS Suffix  . :
        IP Address. . . . . . . . . . . : 0.0.0.0
        Subnet Mask . . . . . . . . . . : 0.0.0.0
        Default Gateway . . . . . . . . :

C:\Documents and Settings\rtidrow.TIDROW>
```

TIPS

What does renewing a DHCP lease actually do?
DHCP is a system for automatically assigning IP numbers to computers on a network. The fastest way to ensure that a computer has a valid IP number is to renew the DHCP lease.

Why do I have two sets of numbers like the ones you show here?
If you have multiple network adapters, such as a broadband modem or even a dial-up modem connection, those will show up as well. However, the ipconfig /release command releases only those IP addresses configured by a DHCP server.

194.170.13.231
192.168.14.201

continued

You can use ipconfig to re-lease and renew the DHCP lease of your computer. The utility can also flush and renew Domain Name Server, or DNS, information, which may restore connectivity on your wireless network. This is handy if you have not been on a specific network for several days or weeks. Sometimes the expiration of your IP address comes and goes when you are not connected to the network.

In the meantime, the address you were using — and that your computer is still configured to use — may have been picked up by another computer on the network. Because only one computer can use an IP address at one time, your computer will not be able to connect to the network. The ipconfig /renew command helps to reestablish a new, unique IP address on your computer.

Renew DHCP Lease with ipconfig *(continued)*

8 Type **ipconfig /renew**.

9 Press Enter.

The Command Prompt window displays the Windows IP Configuration results.

10 Type **ipconfig /flushdns**.

11 Press Enter.

● The DNS cache is successfully flushed.

⓬ Type **ipconfig /registerdns**.

⓭ Press **Enter**.

● Windows XP registers the DNS records for your computer.

⓮ Click the **Close** icon (⊠).

The Command Prompt window closes.

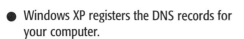

TIPS

How can I view detailed information about my DHCP lease and wireless network adapter?

You can view detailed DHCP information about a network connection by right-clicking the **Network Connection** icon (▣) in the system tray and selecting **Status** from the menu. Click the **Status** tab and then click **Details**.

Does every network have a DHCP server?

No. Some networks assign static IP addresses instead of dynamic ones. Static IP addresses are those that never change on the computer. Instead, the system administrator assigns each computer an IP address and configures that computer with that IP addresses. The downsides to this are many, including the time it takes to set up the IP addresses in the first place. Also, if a computer leaves the network, such as mobile one, it "takes" that IP address away until the administrator assigns it to another computer.

You can see the status of your network by using the `netstat` command. Netstat identifies your network address and other related information. The `netstat` command shows the number of bytes you have received and sent during this network session, how many packets have been received and sent, number of errors, and other information.

Show Network Connections with netstat

① In a Command Prompt window, type **netstat –E**.

Note: For more on opening the Command Prompt window, see the section "Renew DHCP Lease with ipconfig."

② Press Enter.

The Command Prompt window displays interface statistics.

Numbers in both the Received and Sent columns confirm that your wireless network is active.

```
Command Prompt

Microsoft Windows XP [Version 5.1.2600]
(C) Copyright 1985-2001 Microsoft Corp.

C:\Documents and Settings\rtidrow.TIDROW>netstat -E       ①
```

```
Command Prompt

Microsoft Windows XP [Version 5.1.2600]
(C) Copyright 1985-2001 Microsoft Corp.

C:\Documents and Settings\rtidrow.TIDROW>netstat -E
Interface Statistics

                           Received            Sent
Bytes                      17268204         1972943
Unicast packets               18427           17992
Non-unicast packets             192             255
Discards                          0               0
Errors                            0               0
Unknown protocols                12

C:\Documents and Settings\rtidrow.TIDROW>
```

③ Type netstat **-r**.

④ Press **Enter**.

A route table appears.

● The network address of your computer appears.

● Your wireless router or other network gateway address appears.

TIPS

How can I view a list of active connections that my computer has established with other computers?

You can view a list of active connections by using the netstat command. Simply type **netstat** in the Command Promt window and a list of active connections appears.

How can I use this information to troubleshoot my network connections?

One way to use this information is to trace where your computer has gone. That way if you pick up any rogue programs (such as a virus) you may be able to backtrack your path and avoid this resource in the future.

Confirm Connection with pathping

Sometimes you may think you are connected to the network, but you have problems accessing files, receiving e-mail, or running certain network programs. One way to find out if you are actually connected properly is to run a test between your computer and another on the network.

You can run this test either on your wireless network, or on the Internet using the `pathping` **utility.** `pathping` **transmits data packets across the network and measures how long they take to return.**

Confirm Connection with pathping

① In a Command Prompt window, type **pathping** and then the address you want to test.

② Press **Enter**.

pathping displays the route it took to the destination address.

● Your computer appears here.

● The computers between your computer and the destination computer appear here.

● The destination computer appears here.

③ Scroll down to the last entry in the window.

● pathping computes statistics for the connection and displays the results.

Note: *It may take a few minutes for the information to fully display.*

● The destination computer appears here.

● The time required to reach the destination computer appears here in milliseconds.

Note: *If your computer is not connected to a wireless network, pathping shows only your computer in the connection results.*

Can I confirm my network connection without viewing the route the pathping data takes?

Yes. You can use a simpler command-line utility called ping. ping tells you if your computer can reach a destination computer or Internet address, and how long the connection requires. To use the ping utility, type **ping** instead of **pathping** in Step **1**. You must include a destination address after the ping command.

Are there other networking commands I can use?

Yes, there are several that are provided with Windows. In fact, many of the tools that are built with graphical interfaces use many of these commands to return results. A few other commands are tracert, net name, and net view. See the Windows Help and Support Center for more information.

Questions
Answers
Help
Shift + F12
Windows Help

Index

Index

Index

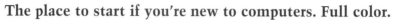

Read Less–Learn More®

There's a Visual book for every learning level...

Simplified®

The place to start if you're new to computers. Full color.

- Computers
- Mac OS
- Office
- Windows

Teach Yourself VISUALLY™

Get beginning to intermediate-level training in a variety of topics. Full color.

- Computers
- Crocheting
- Digital Photography
- Dreamweaver
- Excel

- Guitar
- HTML
- Knitting
- Mac OS
- Office

- Photoshop
- Photoshop Elements
- PowerPoint
- Windows
- Word

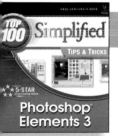

Top 100 Simplified® Tips & Tricks

Tips and techniques to take your skills beyond the basics. Full color.

- Digital Photography
- eBay
- Excel
- Google

- Internet
- Mac OS
- Photoshop

- Photoshop Elements
- PowerPoint
- Windows

Build It Yourself VISUALLY™

Do it yourself the visual way and without breaking the bank. Full color.

- Game PC
- Media Center PC

...all designed for visual learners—just like you!

Master VISUALLY®

Step up to intermediate-to-advanced technical knowledge. Two-color interior.

- 3ds max
- Creating Web Pages
- Dreamweaver and Flash
- Excel VBA Programming
- iPod and iTunes
- Mac OS
- Optimizing PC Performance
- Photoshop Elements
- QuickBooks
- Quicken
- Windows Server
- Windows

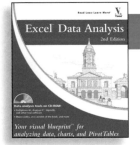

Visual Blueprint™

Where to go for professional-level programming instruction. Two-color interior.

- Excel Data Analysis
- Excel Programming
- HTML
- JavaScript
- PHP

Visual Encyclopedia™

Your A to Z reference of tools and techniques. Full color.

- Dreamweaver
- Photoshop
- Windows

For a complete listing of Visual books, go to wiley.com/go/visualtech

Visual
An Imprint of ⓦW
Now you know